Living in the Light of His Coming

Inspiration and motivation from the Thessalonian Letters

Jim Dick

ISBN: 978-1-907929-89-2

Editing, layout and design by Life Publications
www.lifepublications.org.uk

Author

Jim Dick has been a minister with the Elim Pentecostal Churches for 53 years serving in various roles including as a member of the National Leadership Team, Regional Superintendent of Scotland and Principal of Regents Theological College, but mostly as a pastor in Elim churches including Felixstowe, Cardiff, Kingstanding, Kilsyth and Bristol. He has been married to Margery for 55 years and they currently live in Yate, near Bristol, where they attend the Gateway Elim Church and are part of the pastoral team.

Jim has recently retired from preaching for health reasons so is now able to devote more time to writing.

For more information on his books you can contact Jim by email: jimdick41@gmail.com

Acknowledgments

I would like to pay tribute to Alex Tee, my first Pastor, and the one who introduced me to Second Coming teaching. It was his favourite subject in preaching, so as a young Christian I was well grounded in this truth. Alex has now gone to be with the Lord but I am grateful to God for the years when I sat under his instruction.

I would also record grateful thanks to Ruth Jones for her painstaking proof-reading of the manuscript. Before retiring Ruth was a teacher and I can't help but think that if I had been taught grammar by someone like Ruth there would be far less red marks on this manuscript, so thank you Ruth for your patience and attention to detail.

Grateful thanks once again to Jan and David for the labour of love in producing this book. What they do is not just a job it is a ministry *'as unto the Lord'*.

Enclosed is a copy of my new book: *"Living in the Light of his Coming"*
I think it is the most important book I have written, certainly the most difficult. I hope you will be blessed and challenged by it.
If you would like more copies please contact me. They are £5:99 + postage.

Jim Dick
41 Chatterton Road, Yate, Bristol, BS37 4BJ
Telephone: 01454 322035
Mobile: 07710 487611
Email: jimdick41@gmail.com

Commendations

Jim Dick uses all his experience of life and ministry to put a book into your hands that draws you in, enticing you to turn each new page. World news, fake news, social media have bombarded the synaptic pathways causing an anesthetised overload, leading to a slumber and apathy to cover many a mind's eye. Jim's clear and systematic unravelling of the Second Coming will cause, I believe, an awakening, a much needed refocusing on the individual and collective churches' position and role in these days. A book for the scholar and 'beginner', bringing a refreshing challenge to live wholeheartedly conscious of the days that we live in – you won't be able to put it down!

Martin Davison, Senior Minister
Gateway Revival Church, Yate

Once again Jim Dick expresses himself through excellent writing, this time the content is *The Second Coming*, a subject, sadly, rarely taught in today's church, which is a huge gap in its ministry. Jim brings light, thought and provocatively stimulates the reader to think seriously about preparation for His Coming.

The book delves deeply into Scripture and unpacks Prophecy, the teachings of Jesus and Paul's teachings in the Epistles. This is a deep and thoughtful analysis of *The End of the Age* and will encourage the Church to *"Look up for our Redemption draws near"*.

Geoff Feasey
Former Regional Superintendent
Elim Pentecostal Church UK

Contents

Part 3

Ready for His Appearing

Introduction

Belief and teaching on the return of Jesus to receive His Church and to set up His Kingdom on this earth will have an effect on how we live our lives. It is not a truth just for discussion or debate; it is a truth to be lived out in our daily living. The way we see the future will have an effect on how we live in the present. If we believe that Christ could return at any moment and that our works and the condition of our hearts will be made public for all to see, that will have an effect in how we live each day. The gospel message can be summed up – 'Christ died, Christ rose from the dead, Christ will return'. When belief in the return of Christ is fully grasped it will make us re-evaluate our priorities and teach us how we should prioritise our time, energy and resources.

This book is not written for theologians or eschatological academics but rather for ordinary believers whose everyday lives can so easily become overcrowded with a multitude of activities that drown out time for concentration on life-affecting truths. My hope and desire is that this short book will provide an accessible source of teaching for busy people. Thessalonica is one of my favourite New Testament churches. I will be very pleased if some (all) of the readers of this book will get inspiration and motivation from this remarkable Church.

Paul only had a very short stay in the city of Thessalonica (see Acts 17:1-9), but he laid a good foundation of essential teaching on how to live the Christian life and on how the return of Christ would therefore impact this world. The

Thessalonian converts encountered severe persecution when they followed the Lord but they had been taught how to live in the light of the coming of Christ so they lived their daily lives in the joy of the Holy Ghost.

As we progress through the Thessalonian letters we will encounter truth that can profoundly and positively affect our lives and the Thessalonian Church is a powerful example of how great teaching (on the return of Jesus) produces a remarkable Church.

Jim Dick

Part 1

Thessalonica

The making of a Remarkable Church

The next great event for our world will be the return of Jesus Christ. It will be the most momentous happening in world history since the creation. The entire community of angels in heaven, the cherubim and seraphim, those mysterious beings called 'the living creatures', in fact all of heaven will be involved at his appearing. A great company of the heavenly host was present at His first coming and will be participators at His second coming. Every person who is alive at the time of His return along with everyone born since the beginning of time will stand before God when heaven's accurate record books will be opened and all will be judged. None will escape and there will be no miscarriages of justice. There will be no atheists or agnostics on that day. The critics, sceptics and mockers will be calling on the mountains to cover them and shield them from the righteous wrath of Him who sits on heaven's throne.

This awesome event is imminent – it could happen at any moment. It will be introduced by a trumpet blast from heaven, the voice of an archangel and a loud command from God. This will be the initiation of the finale of God's long-range plan of salvation culminating in the creation of a new earth and new heavens which will be the permanent home of righteousness; it will be the answer to the closing prayer of the Scriptures *"Come Lord Jesus"*.

In the light of these imminent cosmic events it is astonishing that the return of Jesus has such a low place in current preaching and in the conversations of those who believe in His return but are living as if it will not happen for a long time. If we had reliable information that the Lord was going to return at a precise time and day there would be a dramatic rise in personal holiness, witnessing to family members and the resolving of relationship difficulties. All tithes would be up-to-date, the prayer meeting would be packed to the door and the Church would be alive with praise and worship.

My desire in the writing of this short book is to re-awaken focus and attention on His coming – the next and final great event in world history. It will affect every one of us in a profound way. In Romans 13:11-12 Paul gives a strong admonition to those who believe in Christ's return,

> *And do this, understanding the present time, the hour has already come for you to wake up from your slumber, because our salvation is nearer now than when we first believed. The night is nearly over; the day is almost here. So let us put aside the deeds of darkness and put on the armour of light.*

The back-drop for our study will be the letters of Paul to the Thessalonians – two letters that are vitally concerned with Christ's return. The letters, the men who were in leadership at the time, and the members of the remarkable Church at Thessalonica, all have so much to teach us, the twenty-first century followers of Christ.

1st and 2nd Thessalonians were written by the Apostle Paul to the newly formed Church in the city of Thessalonica which was the second Church to be started by Paul in what we now know as Europe.

The first century Churches were plagued by deception and false teachers motivated and instigated by Satan, the arch enemy of the Church, in his unremitting hatred against God. Satan knew that the distortion and pollution of truth would seriously weaken the Church so Paul and all the apostles were engaged in a relentless battle to defend truth. It wasn't long before the peddlers of confusion, the false teachers who had attacked the other Churches, arrived at Thessalonica to continue their satanic work.

At Corinth the false teachers had sought to undermine belief in the resurrection of Christ so the two Corinthian letters, written by Paul, contain some of his best teaching on the subject of the resurrection. In Colossae, the letter to that Church was to present the full sufficiency of Christ in the face of human philosophy. In Thessalonica the false teachers sowed confusion among the new converts on Paul's teaching about the return of Jesus Christ. So again, Paul presents the antidote to this error – solid and reliable teaching on the return of Jesus at the end of the age.

Teaching on the return of Jesus is so often given a back seat to the more popular teachings on prosperity, personal destiny and other 'self' related subjects that fill the air-waves. With the intensity and acceleration of world events, the increasing complexity of world issues and the perplexity of nations at their inability to solve the world's problems, it is undoubtedly time for us to revisit essential New Testament teaching on the return of Christ and what is going to happen when we enter the final chapter of this world's history.

History is not haphazard! God is working to a long-range plan to fully restore all that has been disfigured and ruined by mankind's rebellion and not only to restore but also, with that restoration, to usher in the creation of new heavens and earth that will be the permanent dwelling place of righteousness. It is a big plan, securely resting on the foundation of the death and resurrection of Christ and climaxing at the return of Jesus when the promise of Ephesians 1:9,10 will be fulfilled,

> *...he made known to us the mystery of his will according to his good pleasure, which he purposed in Christ, to be put into effect when the times reach their fulfilment – **to bring unity to all things in heaven and on earth under Christ**.*

Please take the time to read Acts 17 and 1 and 2 Thessalonians.

1st and 2nd Thessalonians, two first century letters, are very relevant for twenty-first century Christians. They contain insights into Christ's return not found anywhere else in the New Testament. In Matthew 24 Jesus uttered the clearest and most pointed warnings concerning three dangers that will confront latter-day followers of Christ.

- He said that because of the rise in ***persecution*** many will turn away from the faith (Matthew 24:9,10)
- He went on to say that because of ***deception*** from false teachers many will be deceived (Matthew 24:11)
- He further warned that because of the increase of ***wickedness*** the love of most will grow cold (Matthew 24:12)

These are sobering words and warnings that should be heeded by every follower of Christ. Sadly, however, many, especially in the Western Hemisphere, are in a dangerously weak condition spiritually. The Thessalonian Christians were familiar with all three of these attacks so their response and Paul's teaching are indispensable for us today.

The Church at Thessalonica

The New Testament contains insights into several first century Churches, each one had its own distinct character.

Antioch was a Church that played a significant part in the spreading of the gospel to the Roman Empire. It was started by Christian refugees fleeing to Antioch from the persecution in Jerusalem that arose after the martyrdom of Stephen. Barnabas was the first Pastor who enlisted the help of the recently converted Saul of Tarsus to help him teach the great crowd of new converts in Antioch.

One of the great features of this Church was the blending together of Jews and Gentiles to form the new 'normal' New Testament Church membership with no social, gender or religious divisions. Once, when the Church was gathered together, along with the leaders, the Holy Spirit spoke and asked them to release Saul and Barnabas to venture into regions untouched by the gospel. This was the start of missions as we now know it.

Later, again from Antioch, Paul (previously called Saul) and Silas were sent on another missionary trip that was to result in the establishing of another highly significant Church that would, like Antioch, play a crucial role in the establishing of the Kingdom of God in the Roman Empire. On this trip, as Paul, Silas and Timothy (who had recently joined them) progressed through regions of the Empire, they became aware of a very strong control from the Holy Spirit regarding the direction they were moving in. They were firmly restrained from entering Asia and Bithynia and finally, while in the city of Troas, Paul received an unambiguous command from the Holy Spirit that they had to head for Macedonia.

The instructions came in the form of a vision of a man from Macedonia who was seen to be pleading with Paul to *'come over and help us'* (Acts 16:9). And so with immediate response, the three men set sail for Macedonia. They landed at Philippi and soon were involved in preaching the good news of God's Kingdom for the very first time in this country. Despite floggings and imprisonment the first Church in mainland Europe was established.

Moving on from Philippi, Paul, Silas and Timothy continued their penetration of Macedonia and deliberately by-passed major cities like Amphipolis and Apollonia, it seemed as though there was an itinerary and a time-table in the Holy Spirit's guiding that was leading the men with laser-like precision to the city of Thessalonica. Little did they know the Holy Spirit was about to establish a significant Church which would have a powerful ripple effect that would expand into far flung corners of the Roman Empire.

In a remarkably short space of time (possibly as short as a few weeks) Paul, Silas and Timothy witnessed and established in the city of Thessalonica, a Church whose influence and reputation penetrated far and wide. What were the ingredients of its success and what can we learn to help 21st century Church in its desire to impact our world in a similar way? The two letters to the Thessalonians have a wealth of great teaching to help us face the challenges of our day, teaching on what authentic leadership, authentic disciples and authentic Churches should look like.

The Importance of 'Church'

In the New Testament a number of metaphors are used to give a picture of what a gathering of God's people should be like. They are referred to as His body, His bride, His army, His building, His temple, His flock, His vine, His family – each one illustrating a feature of our relationship to the Lord and each other.

The word most frequently used in the New Testament to describe God's people when they are together, however, is the word 'Church'. In modern usage it tends to stand for a building used for religious worship, but this association is very far removed from the meaning understood by the early New Testament Christians.

In the first century the word had a secular connotation as well as a spiritual one and at its most basic level, *'Ekklesia' (Church)* meant, 'a gathering', 'an assembly' and could be used in a number of contexts – for instance an assembly of citizens called out from other citizens and gathered together to perform a specific task for the benefit of the city which could be for its defence or a construction project. The Holy Spirit took up this word, which had a well-understood meaning for the early believers, and it began to be used to convey an understanding of the purpose of the gathering together of Christ's disciples in any city or town. It was a word with three distinct features in its meaning – and they provide three essential components of belonging to His Church:

- ***The Call:*** people who are called out from the world by a genuine conversion experience
- ***The Community:*** people who are gathered together – for worship, discipleship and fellowship
- ***The Commission:*** people who have a task to perform – to evangelise and preach His Kingdom

What makes a gathering of God's people different from any other? Jesus said that where two or three of His disciples are gathered together in His name He will be there with them in the centre of their assembly. It is a gathering in His Name with the Lord present among them – that's what makes the difference.

Church is not just a crowd of religious people who happen to be in the same building. Rather, it consists of people who have responded to the call of Jesus, *"Come to me and I will give you rest"* (Matthew 11:28), and by confessing with their mouths that He is Lord they have become a living part of His Kingdom. Called and gathered together but for a distinct purpose – to be trained and equipped to fulfil His commission to go into the entire world so that more people can hear the call and join the gathering.

Church consists of people who are called out from the world, gathered together in His name and committed to the greatest task in the world – advancing His Kingdom, doing His will and glorifying the name of the Lord. For some people Church has a bad reputation and have left it – disillusioned and disappointed by its failure to provide spiritual life. It is my hope and prayer that this study of the Thessalonian letters will help us rediscover the power of real Church as Christ intended it to be.

We are now in the 21st century and two thousand years closer to the coming of the Lord than the first century Christians were but sadly, rather than this fact driving the Church to greater effort in world evangelisation, it is a sobering fact that large sections of the Church are woefully ill-prepared for the promised return of our Saviour. The true meaning of Church has been lost in a deluge of alternative interests that finds many Churches very busy but not necessarily employing time, resources and energy in advancing the Kingdom of God. This short book will be an attempt to re-discover *"Church as **He** wants it"*. We have had *"Church as **we** want it"* for long enough. It is time for change. The biblical back-drop will be Paul's first and second letters to the Thessalonians, both written to one of the most remarkable Churches in the New Testament. In the letters to the Thessalonians we will encounter teaching that will help shape our lives, individually and as Churches, to make us fit and ready for the momentous challenges of the final days of human history and prepare us to meet our returning Lord with joy and confidence. We will learn about:

- The clearest definition of the evidences of an authentic new-birth experience
- A precise description of the behaviour that should accompany a new-birth experience
- The authentic life style and conduct of effective leaders
- The astonishing effect that one poverty-stricken Church had on the Roman Empire
- Teaching about the return of Jesus that is not found anywhere else in the New Testament
- Paul's unique understanding of three aspects of the last days just before Christ's return: the great rebellion, the emergence of the Man of Lawlessness (the Antichrist) and the perpetration of 'The Lie' – the biggest lie in history which will deceive many
- What Christian fellowship should be like in days of rising opposition and hostility and how believers can prepare themselves to face the most momentous days in world history
- The effect that an understanding of Christ's return should have on every disciple of Christ
- How to live and witness with joyful confidence

The Features of a Powerful Church

Thessalonica was a significant and highly effective Church and we will find out shortly, just how this Church, despite its extreme poverty and vicious persecution, impacted the world of its day. How do you measure a Church's success or effectiveness? Today we are impressed by the size of the congregation, the conclusion being that if so many are attending it must be doing something right. We are also impressed by 'state-of-the-art' premises with very comfortable seats, good car parking, safe crèche facilities and cutting-edge media technology using hugely expensive sound systems that fully present the musicians and singers. The Church's weekly programme will cater for every need and the welcome process will be well planned and impressive. Today's successful Church will usually have a leader who travels widely to preach at large gatherings and who is not too old to wear skinny jeans and who has a wide range of books, CDs, DVDs and other means of mass communication on sale at the end of every service.

Thessalonica would not pass on any of the above criteria but listen to the story of their remarkable transformation when they received Christ into their lives. The story went viral!

> *You welcomed the message (of Christ) in the midst of severe suffering with the joy given by the Holy Spirit. And so you became a model to all the believers in Macedonia and Achaia. The Lord's message rang out from you not only in Macedonia and Achaia – your faith in God has become known everywhere. Therefore, we do not need to say anything about it, for they themselves report what kind of reception you gave us. They tell how you turned to God from idols to serve the living and true God, and to wait for his Son from heaven,*

whom He raised from the dead – Jesus, who rescues us from the coming wrath.

1 Thessalonians 1:6-10

Wow! What a testimony. It went beyond the city boundaries, way beyond the district, even into surrounding countries – the remarkable story of people who enthusiastically embraced Christ and wanted the world to know that Christ could be their Saviour and transform every life.

Churches come in all shapes and condition, from the very ordinary and ineffective right through to an exceptional one like Thessalonica. There are two factors that contributed to making Thessalonica into such a world affecting Church:

1. ***The members***: Take note of the radical and uncompromising reception the Thessalonians gave to the gospel. There were no half measures or compromise for they had come to understand that Christ sacrificed all for them so no sacrifice for Him was too great. Their totally revolutionised lives were talked about in far flung parts of the Empire. The gospel of Christ received an enthusiastic and wholehearted response from these ex pagans.

2. ***The leaders:*** Take note the unapologetic and courageous presentation of the good news of Christ that Paul, Silas and Timothy gave to the citizens of Thessalonica - the proclamation of the message was accompanied by power, the Holy Ghost and deep conviction. This was this backed up by the exemplary lives of the missionaries.

The song of Deborah in Judges 5:2 sums up the world-affecting power of this wonderful combination – good leaders and a willing people,

> *When the princes in Israel take the lead, when the people willingly offer themselves – praise the Lord!*
>
> Judges 5:2

Leaders and people willing and united in obedience to Christ – indeed a cause for praise to God.

We will now look at these two 'success' factors a little more closely.

(1) The Converts

There are three ways that Christ is fully presented to the world:

1. ***By proclamation*** – words which people hear. This can be achieved by the giving of a personal testimony about what the Lord has done in an individual life. It is important for every follower of Christ to know how to present the story of their conversion. Telling the story of your journey to Christ is one of the most effective forms of evangelism and also the cheapest.

   Words are also used by the preacher to present the good news of Christ's salvation. Paul very effectively employed words in presenting Christ. Look at the four different 'styles' he used in preaching at Thessalonica; *"He **reasoned** with them from the Scriptures, he **explained** and he **proved** that Christ had to suffer and be raised from the dead….this is the Jesus I am **proclaiming** to you,"* (Acts 17:2,3). This would be done by means of discourse, questions and answers and a reasoned laying out in order of the gospel story.

2. ***By demonstration*** – signs, wonders, and miracles. This is what people feel. Paul reminded the Thessalonians of how the gospel first came to them; *"Our gospel came to you not simply with words but also with power, with the Holy Spirit and deep conviction,"* (1 Thessalonians 1: 5).

3. ***By illustration*** – transformed lives. This is what people see. Few of us are academics and theologians like Paul so you might not be able to answer every question but you are an authority on your life and the transformation that Christ has made in you can speak volumes.

When people hear a verbal presentation of the gospel which is backed up by the experience of God's power at work and further validated by changed lives, then they are being convincingly and attractively offered an opportunity to receive God's way of salvation through Christ.

When Paul, Silas and Timothy came to Thessalonica they first went to the Jewish synagogue and for three Sabbaths they preached about Christ (see Acts 17:2,3). The message attracted some but angered others. There were converts – some of the Jews responded plus a large number of God-fearing Greeks and quite a few of the city's prominent women. But other Jews became very angry, prompted by jealousy, at the success of the gospel and no doubt they were enraged at Paul's presentation of an inclusive gospel which put women and Gentiles on an equal footing before God. Soon a very large number of citizens were committed to Christ and such was the radical nature of their life-transforming conversion, that the news began to circulate in the city and further afield. Before we look at the distinctive evidences of their conversion, we need to understand a little of the city and the culture of Thessalonica.

The city and culture they lived in

'The Egnatian Way' which was a main highway running from Constantinople to Rome, and Thessalonica was positioned on this vital travel artery for the Roman Empire. Merchants and travellers constantly traversed it and people from every part of the Empire poured into the city to find accommodation and food before they continued on their journey. So when the radical Christian converts began to fill the city with the message of Christ the travellers had a story to tell when they moved on to every part of Empire.

The city had been well chosen by the Holy Spirit and became like a spiritual hub that radiated out and soon news of the transformed lives of the converts reached all of Macedonia, into Achaia and beyond. Paul and his companions were not able to spend a lot of time in the city (it could have been as short as three weeks, it wasn't a lot more) but such was the radical transforming power of the gospel presented by the anointing of the Spirit that the results were out-of-proportion to the short crusade.

It wasn't long before violent hostility broke out and the Jewish opposition soon rented a mob. The apostles were forced to leave the city and move on to Berea and the new converts were left without their leaders. How would they survive? They had only been saved for a few weeks, but they had been well taught. When Timothy later returned from a trip to check on them with the news that they were standing firm for Christ, the concern of the leaders was dispelled and they were filled with joy. Not only were they remaining firm but were advancing.

In the story of the Thessalonian Church we learn the great power of the gospel, not only to *save* us but also to *keep* us. The Thessalonian converts faced a firestorm of determined opposition and persecution which had repercussions in their financial lives. Following Christ cost them dearly but the sacrifice was made with great joy:

> *You welcomed the message in the midst of* ***severe*** *suffering with the joy given by the Holy Spirit... no one should be unsettled by these trials. For you know quite well that we were destined for them. In fact, when we were with you, we kept telling you that we would be persecuted. And it turned out that way, as you well know...we want you to know about the grace God has given the Macedonian Churches. In the midst of a* ***very severe trial****, their overflowing and their* ***extreme poverty*** *welled up in rich generosity.*
>
> 1 Thessalonians 1:6; 3:3,4
> and 2 Corinthians 8:1,2

Paul's teaching and the experience of the Thessalonian Christians were exactly in line with what Jesus had taught His disciples,

> *Blessed are those who are persecuted because of righteousness, for theirs is the Kingdom of heaven. Blessed are you when people insult you, persecute you and falsely say all kinds of evil against you because of me. Rejoice and be glad, because great is your reward in heaven.*
>
> *Matthew 5:10-12*

Luke's account of this sermon adds,

> *Blessed are you when people hate you, when they exclude you and insult you and reject your name as evil, because of the Son of Man. Rejoice in that day and leap for joy because great is your reward in heaven.*
>
> Luke 6:22,23

Many Christians today would identify very closely with these conditions and would find comfort and encouragement from the experience of the Thessalonian Christians. Those of us who live in the relatively easy conditions of the Western Hemisphere should take instruction and guidance from our first century brothers and sisters, especially as we see the climate against following Christ, rapidly cooling.

The world does not take kindly to those who live differently from it and the new life-style of the Thessalonian converts was so dramatically different from the culture of the day that, while many were impressed and attracted by it, others were angered by it and determined to eradicate it.

The life revolution that followed conversion for these first century believers contrasted dramatically with that of the Greek Roman culture. There was an obvious difference in how Christians treated children, slaves, women and their attitude to marriage. In the hierarchy of the day adult males were at the top of society and women, slaves and children were at the bottom. The gospel, taught by the apostles, was one where all people, regardless of gender, age or any other distinction, were of equal value to God. The society of the day could abandon the poor to begging on the streets or to prostitution any unwanted children, especially girls. The most barbaric things were done to children in the brothel/prostitution system of the day, some would even be deliberately crippled so they could be made into beggars. It became apparent very quickly that this new alternative society called ‘Christians’ lived lives that were dramatically different to those of the day and it attracted admiration and anger.

So it was a dramatic story of a new radical, Christian, alternative culture flourishing in Thessalonica that the travellers and merchants carried with them as they moved on from the city.

Every Church has a reputation but not all are God-glorifying. Laodicea's reputation was of being lukewarm in their commitment to Christ, Ephesus lost its first-love and others were reputed to be tolerating false teaching but Thessalonica's reputation was, that despite severe persecution and poverty, they stood tall for Christ and wanted all to know it.

> *The Lord's message rang out from you, not only in Macedonia and Achaia – your faith has become known everywhere therefore we do not need to say anything, for they themselves report what kind of reception you gave us. They tell how you turned to God from idols to serve the living and true God, and to wait for his Son from heaven, whom He raised from the dead – Jesus who rescues us from the coming wrath.*
>
> 1 Thessalonians 1:8-10

"Rang out from you" – a great noise, like a thunderclap, like the sound of loud trumpets. This was no shy retiring Church nervous about giving offence or upsetting some people. It was no wonder they experienced opposition and persecution. They were dangerous and, despite 'severe' persecution, they were undeterred and unashamed in their witness to Christ. Sadly, the witness of the Church today is often weakened and devalued by the unclear testimony of the lives of many members.

Compromised lifestyles do not enhance the message of Christ. In Titus 2:10 Paul encouraged Christian slaves to live exemplary lives that would, *"make the teaching about God our Saviour attractive"* – the power of the gospel presented by words but also seen in changed lives. This Church at Thessalonica had a God-glorifying reputation and it wasn't about its programme, its premises or a powerful personality in the pulpit – it was a testimony about the change that had happened in the lives of the converts since receiving Christ as Saviour. The gospel, first and foremost, changes lives. If there is no change there has been no conversion experience. The more clear-cut the change, the more glory there is to God.

Thessalonica was an amazing Church and the testimony of the changed lives of the converts reached far beyond the city boundaries. Shortly, we will look at the second success 'factor' in the Thessalonica Church – *'The quality of its leadership'*, but first a look at the evidences of the new-birth that Paul observed in the Thessalonian converts.

Chapter one of 1 Thessalonians contains what the Reformer John Calvin called 'a brief definition of Christianity' – the three greatest evidences of the new-birth experience. They were also the three big talking points by the merchants as they 'gossiped' the news of the events in this large important Roman city.

The three evidences of the new birth

True conversion is a life-transforming experience; it is not just making some improvements to a person's life or offering suggestions to enhance the quality of life. The New Testament conversion experience is radical and total; it is likened to death and resurrection – death to an old sinful, self-centred way of life and coming alive to a new Christ-centred life. Conversion deals with the past life, the present life and the future.

In 1 Thessalonians 1:3 Paul speaks of:

1. *"Your work produced by **faith**"* (our past)
2. *"Your labour prompted by **love**"* (our present)
3. *"Your endurance inspired by **hope**"* (our future)

Linking verse 3 with verses 9 and 10 of 1 Thessalonians might help in our understanding:

- **The work of faith is to turn to God from idols**

We are saved by faith, not by works but the work of faith will be evident by our works and the great work of faith is to turn away from idols. We cannot turn to God unless we turn away from sin. We cannot face in two directions. There will always be visible evidence when there is a work of the Holy Spirit in a person's life.

The immorality and darkness of the idolatry in Thessalonica was well known so when the Christian converts turned their backs on all that went with the old life controlled by idols, their new allegiance to Christ was obvious for all to see – neighbours and families would observe a radical change in life-style and attitudes.

The work God looks for as an evidence of Holy Spirit activity is when a person turns away from all the 'God-substitutes' which previously filled the life. This change for the Thessalonians had major repercussions – severe suffering and hostility followed by extreme poverty. Not all were attracted by the message of Christ, many were angered, especially the leaders of the Synagogue who stirred up violent hostility against the preachers and the converts; but it was received by the disciples with great joy from the Holy Ghost. Paul speaks very strongly against these religious leaders who should have responded to the truth of the gospel but instead fought to destroy it and hinder people from receiving the message (see 1 Thessalonians 2:13–16).

Once, on a trip to Thailand to visit Elim Missionaries, Tony and Ursula Wilson, I was taken on a tour of a temple. I was intrigued by a room which was really a kind of supermarket where idols of all kinds were on display for sale – idols of wood, stone and metal including gold. Some were very plain, others very ornate. You could browse, and then make your choice of an idol that offered fertility, prosperity, health etc. After paying the price you would take it home, set it up and it was open for worship.

For us today, it may not be idols of stone, wood or metal but the life-controlling God-substitutes of ambition, greed, career, sport, sex, music, a relationship, money, power, alcohol, drugs, gluttony etc. Anything that takes first place in a person's life is an idol. Receiving Christ as Saviour and Lord will mean a radical change of allegiance and a turning away from an old self-centred way of life. The 'turning' will be visible for all to see.

The citizens of the city of Thessalonica certainly took note of the change in life and life-style of the new followers of Christ. There was a clear and unmistakeable contrast between their life before conversion and their life after conversion. It was seen in their love for each other, their marriages and home-life and their treatment of the marginalised sections of society. This was not good works to impress God and gain forgiveness but works that were the evidence of a new life of faith in God.

- **The labour prompted by love is to serve the living and true God**

The writer John Stott said, *"To turn to God from idols is manifestly bogus if it does not result in serving the God to whom we have turned"*.

Love is a powerful evidence of the new birth but this is not just human love, it is extraordinary love for God, for fellow believers and for the lost. Love of sin is replaced by love of service. We are set free to serve God and in serving Him we will serve others. The greatest servant is Christ, so in turning to God, we can only become more like Him.

> *The love of God is shed abroad in our hearts by the Holy Ghost.*
>
> Romans 5:5

> *We are taught by God to love one another.*
>
> 1 Thessalonians 4:9

- **The endurance inspired by hope is to wait for His Son from heaven**

I remind you of the sobering words of Jesus in Matthew 24 when He declared that because of wickedness, deception and persecution, the love of most (followers of Christ) will grow cold, many will depart from the faith and many will be deceived. The effective antidote to these dangerous responses is to live in the daily expectation of Christ's return. There is no uncertainty or doubt accompanying the promise of His coming. It is a sure and certain hope for we have His promise that He will return and just as surely that He came the first time and also that He rose from the grave after His death, so He will certainly come the second time. Believers who are filled with this confident expectancy will endure until He comes. But as we wait, we work – waiting and working. The two are not incompatible – in fact they complement each other. Waiting is not passive, it is active. We work while we wait, so that if we are not engaged in the work of His Kingdom, we are not waiting properly.

We need to remember that we are not waiting for an event – we are waiting for a person – the coming of Jesus Christ, our Saviour and Lord. Verse 10 declares that His resurrection is the guarantee that He will return to gather His Church to Himself. This is not an uncertain hope but a joyful certainty underwritten by His resurrection and these three irrefutable evidences in our lives:

1. In ***faith*** we have turned to God after turning our backs on all the God-substitutes that dominated our lives. God has become the centre of our lives and it is manifestly obvious by a clear-cut change of life and life-style.

2. Our lives are marked by service that is motivated by ***love*** for the living and true God.

3. There is the patient consistency of a God-glorifying life that is inspired by the confident ***hope*** of His return.

The Church in Thessalonica wasn't a mediocre one and its reputation was due in part to the quality of the members who were a credit to the power of the gospel to save and change a person. The Thessalonian converts were very responsive to the teaching of the apostles, they were courageous in their obedience to God, they quickly learned the blessing of generosity and they understood their responsibility to spread the gospel,

> *"...when you received the Word of God which you received from us, you accepted it, not as a human word, but as it actually is, the Word of God, which is indeed at work in you who believe."*
>
> 1 Thessalonians 2:13

Now, as a continuation of our examination of the features of an effective Church, we will look at the contribution that Paul, Silas and Timothy made to the founding of this remarkable Church.

(2) The Leaders

Under the guidance of the Holy Spirit, Paul very carefully, made the choice of the city of Thessalonica; he by-passed other cities to get to this one because he would have been aware of its strategic location and that it was a key to linking the East and the West of the Roman Empire. It was called 'the lap of the Empire'. Traders from every part of the Empire poured in and out of the city scattering to all the corners of the Empire. So with the gospel well established in this city the message could be disseminated to the Roman Empire throughout the Egnatian Way.

It must have been a major blow to Paul, Silas and Timothy when, after a very short stay, they were forced, because of very hostile opposition, to leave and move on to Berea. The converts they were forced to leave were so young in the faith. How would they survive? Would the Church disappear? Many questions would have filled their minds and such was Paul's concern that he eventually sent Timothy back to enquire after their welfare. When Timothy returned with the good news of their steadfastness, the miracle of Holy Ghost power to save and protect was soon in evidence (see 1 Thessalonians 3:5,6). The Church not only survived but, despite extreme persecution, it flourished and soon the testimony of changed lives was beginning to 'filter out' on the lips of the traders, to the corners of the Empire.

As I write this I am reminded of the example of the Church in China:

The miraculous growth of the Chinese Church

Robert Morrison was one of the first Missionaries in 1807. The Captain of the ship he came on said to him as he landed, 'do you really expect to make a difference on the idolatry of the great Chinese Empire'? His answer, 'No sir, but I expect God will'.

After seven years he baptised his first convert and prayed – 'may he be the first fruits of a great harvest, of millions who shall believe.'

Hudson Taylor came and hundreds of others and after 150 years of hard work there were about 700,000 Protestant believers.

Then came the Cultural Revolution and the Bamboo Curtain came down and the last Western missionary was expelled in 1953. The China watchers thought they would have to go in and start all over again – they heard news of savage persecution, church buildings all destroyed, Bibles burned and all leaders imprisoned and cruelly treated, all religious props removed. Would anyone survive?

After almost thirty years of silence, the doors began to slowly open and news began to filter out of a mighty miracle not only of preservation but of dramatic expansion. The fire had not destroyed it but rather refined it.

Today the estimates of 100 million Christians and 30,000 getting saved each day are not exaggerated. The South China Post published an article stating that there are 125 million

Christians in China and there are more Christians than members of the Communist Party.

We are examining the dynamic combination of good leadership and responsive followers. I remind you of that illuminating verse from Judges 5 that I quoted earlier,

"...when the princes (leaders) in Israel take the lead, when the people willing offer themselves – praise the Lord!"

We have seen the willing response of the new converts at Thessalonica but now we will examine the qualities of Paul's leadership. In the Thessalonian letters, you cannot miss the overflowing pastoral heart of the Apostle:

- His passion for the work he was involved in
- His in-depth prayers for the Church
- His personal integrity and life-example
- His unflinching courage in the face of opposition
- His unwavering commitment to the converts

We will examine four aspects of Paul's leadership – his preaching, his integrity, his pastoral care and teaching and his prayers.

1. Paul's preaching

Paul, Silas and Timothy were in Macedonia by the will and purpose of God. But from the start of their evangelism they were met by severe opposition and persecution. In Philippi they were stripped, beaten and thrown into prison. In Thessalonica, it was much the same when a mob started a riot making it necessary for the apostles to move on to Berea. The gospel of inclusion that Paul preached incensed the Jewish Synagogue leaders and constantly brought Paul into conflict with them wherever he went.

I spoke earlier of the three ways that Christ is fully presented: by proclamation (what people hear); by demonstration (what people feel); and by illustration (what people see in changed lives). Through Paul's preaching, all three evidences were in operation in Thessalonica.

In 1 Thessalonians 1:4,5 Paul reminded the converts of his ministry among them,

> *"Our gospel came to you not simply with words but also with power, with the Holy Spirit and deep conviction. You know how we lived among you for your sake."*

There was a presentation of the gospel by *"reasoning, explaining, proving and proclaiming"* (Acts 17:2,3). This was accompanied by a demonstration of miracle power by the Holy Spirit and the new disciples had wonderful illustrations of the Christian life as shown in the three apostles.

Paul adopted the same method of gospel presentation in Corinth,

> *"My message and preaching were not with wise and persuasive words, but with the demonstration of the Spirit's power, so that your faith might not rest on human wisdom but on God's power."*
>
> 1 Corinthians 2:4

A careful study of the Acts of the Apostles will show that the majority of the miracles recorded there were in the context of evangelism. In China's house churches it is estimated that as many as 80 per cent of believers first came to Jesus because they received a miraculous healing or deliverance from the Lord.

When Paul speaks of 'deep conviction' (v5), it is not so much the effect of the Word on the listeners but rather the force of the Word in the preacher. Paul was totally convinced that the gospel was the power of God for salvation and regardless of his audience, he was unapologetic in his presentation of Christ.

2. *Paul's personal integrity*

In 1 Thessalonians 2 we get a glimpse into the heart of the apostle and we see the emotions and pain a true leader will go through to accomplish the purpose of God in people's lives. We also get a look into the malevolent hearts of his opponents.

He had enraged the religious establishment by his presentation of an inclusive gospel that placed women, slaves and Gentiles on an equal footing with Jews before God. They were unrelenting in their hatred. They hounded Paul for the rest of his life and were persistent in their attacks on the Churches he established. They had a simple plan of attack against Paul – 'discredit the messenger, discredit the message'.

They ceaselessly attacked Paul's character and integrity by spreading rumours and lies about what he was teaching and undermined his motivation. They said Paul was only doing it for what he could get out of it and that he was after their money, that he was a failure, that he was deluded and was out of his mind. Paul responds to some of the accusations, not to defend his character or reputation, but for the sake of the converts and the integrity of the gospel.

- Paul defends his *message* (see 1 Thessalonians 2:1) – the message did not fail; it produced results and the Thessalonians were those results.
- Paul defends his *motives* (see 1 Thessalonians 2:3,4) – they were not based on greed, nor was it to gain a reputation.
- Paul defends his *methods* (see 1 Thessalonians 2:5) – he never resorted to trickery, or used flattery or put on a mask of pretence – no manipulative methods. His life was transparent before God and so was equally transparent before people.

In 1 Thessalonians 2:14–16 his anger, at the damage the Judaisers were doing to new converts, boils over. The language he uses is strong – *"they killed the Lord Jesus, they killed the prophets, they drove the apostles out, they displease God, they are hostile to all men"*. These Judaisers had access to the truth but rejected it and worse still, they were hindering others from receiving the truth and he rounds it off with,

> *"They displease God...in their efforts to keep us from speaking to the gentiles so that they may be saved. In this way they heap up their sins to the limit. The wrath of God has come upon them at last."*
>
> 1 Thessalonians 2:15b–16

In contrast to what the Judaisers were saying Paul and the other evangelists lived exemplary lives before the converts so that they had good role-models to look to as examples of Christian living,

> *"You know how we lived among you for your sake."*
>
> 1 Thessalonians 1:3

> *"....You are witnesses, and so is God, of how holy, righteous and blameless we were among you who believed."*
>
> 1 Thessalonians 2:10

People are affected as much by what they see as by what they hear.

We have been looking at the factors that contribute to an effective leader and so far we have examined the importance of preaching and personal integrity. There are two more that are obvious in the Thessalonian letters.

3. Paul's pastoral care and teaching

Paul may only have been in Thessalonica for a relatively short time but the new converts had carved a big place in his heart. His two letters to them, after he left, are wonderful examples of his pastoral heart. In 1 Thessalonians 2 Paul uses three metaphors to describe his loving care for them:

1. ***As a steward*** – *"We speak as men* ***approved*** *by God to be* ***entrusted*** *with the gospel" (v4).*

   Becoming an apostle was not a career move for Paul nor was it a means to gain position, power or financial reward. Paul saw himself as a steward in God's household. He owned nothing for himself but was faithful in caring for all that belonged to God. During many years of training Paul had been tested by God and proved that he could be trusted with Christian stewardship. He was not in the ministry for personal advancement, he was no silver-tongued salesman using manipulative methods to get results, his methods were always in keeping with the message, and he carried God's stamp of approval.

2. ***As a mother*** – *"We were gentle among you as a mother caring for her little children" (v7).*

   Paul was tough, rugged, strong and not afraid to suffer but he did not shrink from using this feminine metaphor on himself (see Numbers 11:12–15 where this metaphor is applied to Moses with Israel). Paul's accusers said he was a dictator but the converts knew the truth about the way he cared for them. A mother plays such a vital role in the care of new babies – she gives the baby its first food and is very careful of what she herself eats knowing that it will be turned into nutritious milk for her child. She is responsible for teaching the basic life-skills – how to eat, walk, dress, wash, good behaviour, manners etc. She is responsible for protection when the infant is at its most vulnerable and will gladly give her life for the child. A mother is very patient with the new child and is usually the one who clears up its mess. Paul displayed all of these characteristics to his precious converts.

3. ***As a father*** – *"We dealt with each of you as a father deals with his own children" (v11).*

   Father love is different from mother love. It is not inferior or superior just different. Paul brings out three ingredients of a father's role in the care of his children:

   - His work. Paul's accusers said he was only in this for what he could get out of them but he reminds the young converts of his hard work when he was with them – *"We worked night and day in order not to be a burden to anyone while we preached the gospel to you".*

- His walk – *"You are witnesses, and so is God, of how holy righteous and blameless we were among you who believe."* Paul didn't just tell them how to live the Christian life, he showed them by personal example, allowing them to get up close and observe how he lived. He wasn't a remote leader who could only be seen at a distance on a platform and isolated by protective paid staff.

- His words – *"encouraging, comforting and urging you to live lives worthy of God".* A father's words are important; they contribute to the laying of a foundation for the child's future security and self-worth. Paul knew how to put courage in them to live openly for God and by comforting words he would give them the will to pick themselves up after failure and go on to succeed. By the use of encouraging words, a son can live successfully, motivated by his father's approval and not constantly trying to win it.

Paul was aware that the new converts needed good teaching but that it had to be accompanied by good parenting. Spiritual fathers (and mothers) are so needed (and so rare) in the Church,

> *"Even though you have ten thousand teachers in Christ you do not have many fathers."*
>
> 1 Corinthians 4:15

Spiritual parents will co-operate in raising healthy offspring – the mother may teach the child to walk physically but the father is needed to teach the child to walk morally. These metaphors – steward, mother and father underline the necessity of a variety of styles of leaders in caring for a Church.

The overall purpose of Paul's influence as steward, mother and father was so that they would, *"live lives worthy of God who calls you into his Kingdom and glory"*. There is no doubting his deep love for his sons and daughters in Christ – his grief when he was torn away from them (v17), his distress when Satan hindered him returning to them (v18) and his overwhelming joy when Timothy arrived back with the report that they were standing firm for Christ despite extreme suffering (3:6–8). His love and joy shine through in his moving prayer for them in 3:9–11.

The teaching Paul gave in that 'oh-so-short' period of time with them was thorough, relevant and practical. Paul follows his usual pattern in writing – teaching and then a life-related application of that teaching. The main teaching he emphasises in the Thessalonian letters is the return of Christ followed up by how they should be living in the light of His coming. His teaching had a clear purpose,

> *"We instructed you how to live in order to please God."*
>
> 1 Thessalonians 4:1

The Christian's greatest motivation for holy living is love not fear, 'Does this please God?' should be the test of all our attitudes and actions (see 1 Thessalonians 2:4). Jesus lived to please His Father and when He stood in the Jordan at His baptism, after spending 30 years of preparation in the despised town of Nazareth, heaven was *'torn open'* and His Father spoke,

> *"You are my Son, whom I love, with you I am* ***well-pleased****."*
>
> Luke 3:22

With Jesus as our great example we must all aspire to live lives that please God and not succumb to the flexible, chameleon-like ethics that characterise so many professing Christians today.

1 Thessalonians 4 is a teaching section where Paul gives instruction on areas of living – they had to be radically different from the people of the world. Paul made it clear that while godly living will save us from judgment, it will not save us from persecution. People who live differently from the world will attract opposition but he goes on to say,

> *"Don't be unsettled by these trials, we were destined for them."*
>
> 1 Thessalonians 3:3

Persecution, for the Thessalonians, would include jail, confiscation of possessions, mistreatment, exclusion etc. Paul taught that receiving the good news must lead to living the good life and that this would inevitably lead to the persecuted life.

Paul was aware that the Thessalonians were already living lives that pleased God but he encouraged them to greater efforts,

> *"We urge you in the Lord Jesus to do this **more** and **more**."*
>
> 1 Thessalonians 4:1

Paul's teaching would cover morals for singles and married members, Church life and work life.

- ***Standards in Morality*** (1 Thessalonians 4:3-6) love, sex and marriage are high on most people's agenda but it is God's will that His people should live by a higher standard from that of the world. The Roman Empire in general and Thessalonica in particular was mired in sexual immorality. The religions of the city were steeped in prostitution, so worship in the temples would include sexual involvement with the priestesses who were also prostitutes.

At the time of my writing this section, the world's media is clogged with multiple stories of immoral behaviour in sport, the film industry, boarding schools and well known charities, leaving multitudes of permanently damaged lives. The teaching of God is for godly restraint and order outside and inside marriage. Paul taught, *"Avoid sexual immorality"* – we are to keep a very clear gap between the standards of the world and those of the Lord's people. Paul does not mince his words,

> *"Each of you should learn to control his own body in a way that is holy and honourable and not in passionate lust like the heathen who do not know God."*
>
> 1 Thessalonians 4:4,5

Lust is not the same as love – lust will use a person to get satisfaction whereas love is sensitive to the needs of the other partner and wants to *give,* not just *get*. The climate within a Christian marriage should be that of respect, holiness, giving, cherishing and honouring – *"no one should wrong or take advantage" (v6)* – no crossing of boundaries of practice into conduct that may make the other partner feel uncomfortable. Paul's word on this topic is strong – *"For God did not call us to be impure but to live a holy life" (v7).* Not to submit to this moral life-style is to reject the command of God,

> *"...anyone who rejects this instruction does not reject a human being but God, the very God who gives you his Holy Spirit."*
>
> 1 Thessalonians 5:8

This 'politically correct' world has hijacked the word 'marriage' and turned it into something very far removed from God's original design. This challenges the followers of Christ to understand the pattern of God's plan and design and to live it out in practice. His plan was for one man and one women to be united by a life-long covenant in a heterosexual relationship and that this intimate, loving union was to be a foretaste and example of the union of Christ and His Church. Paul describes Christian marriage as,

> *"...a profound mystery, but I am talking about Christ and the Church."*
>
> Ephesians 5:32

It is clear that a homosexual relationship between two men or two women can never be a representation of the relationship of Christ and His Church and so cannot have God's approval.

- ***Standards in Church life***

> *"Now about your love for one another we do not need to write to you, for you yourselves have been taught by God to love each other. And in fact, you do love all of God's family throughout all of Macedonia. Yet we urge you, brothers and sisters, to do so more and more."*
>
> 1 Thessalonians 5:9-11

How we behave in Church is important because we are being observed, not just by people on earth but also by those in the heavenlies (see Ephesians 3:10). The love that the Christians had for each other was one of the features that the visiting merchants and travellers spoke about far and wide. Jesus said that *"by this all men will know that you are my disciples, because you love one another"*. Our teacher is God who *"**so** loved the world..."* Love for fellow believers is an indispensable evidence of the new birth,

> *"We know that we have passed from death to life because we love our brothers. Whoever does not love remains in death. Anyone who hates his brother is a murderer and you know that no murderer has eternal life in him."*
>
> 1 John 3:14,15

Although Paul says that the Thessalonians do not need instruction in the subject of love, he goes on to challenge them *"...we urge you, brothers and sisters to do so more and more"*. In his later second letter he declares that they were indeed doing just that, *"your faith is growing more and more, and the love you have for one another is increasing"* (2 Thessalonians 1:3). His prayer was being answered.

- ***Standards in work life*** (1 Thessalonians 4:11,12).

Every part of our lives is sacred to God and part of our worship of God. We cannot divide our lives up into sacred and secular, all of life is sacred and this includes our work life. Some of the converts in Thessalonica were misusing the teaching Paul had given about Christ's return and were using it as an excuse for giving up work – "we will be leaving shortly, so going to work is a waste of time, let's just get excited about our exit and start the party now". The possibility of Christ's imminent return had become an excuse for not working,

> *"...warn those who are idle...we command you to keep away from every brother who is idle and does not live according to the teaching you received from us."*
>
> 1 Thessalonians 5:14 and 2 Thessalonians 3:6

Paul says that they are to be rebuked not just corrected. He is *not* referring to those who cannot work – the rebuke is for those who *will not* work and were misusing Bible teaching to excuse their idleness. A Christian's responsible attitude and good standards towards daily work can be a means of glorifying God and, following the example of our Lord who spent 18 years as a carpenter in Nazareth with no public ministry, sermons or miracles. He gained high commendation from His Father when His unseen years in Nazareth were assessed at the Jordan – *"This is my Son, I love Him, I am pleased with Him"*. Paul issues three admonitions about work to the Thessalonians:

1. *"Make it your ambition to lead a quiet life" (4:11)* – some were getting into a state of feverish excitement about their imminent departure to heaven but Paul wants to dampen down this misdirected enthusiasm and re-channel it to a more productive life-style. High emotion and excitement is often the required atmosphere for many conferences and services but these alone will not produce much that advances the Kingdom of God. Our main ambition should be to please

God in every aspect of our lives not just get excited. This life-style would be in line with the example that Paul, Silas and Timothy gave when they were with them – 2 Thessalonians 3:7-11.

2. *"Mind your own business" (4:11)* and 2 Thessalonians 3:11-15. The disruptive members, because they were not being busy in the right things, had become busybodies in the wrong things – they were meddling in other people's business and were disturbing the peace and harmony of the fellowship with unhelpful gossip and opinions.

3. *"Work with your hands"* – work was not a part of the curse in the Garden of Eden, but toil and sweat were. The Greek philosophy of Paul's day despised manual labour but our Lord, by His own example, has forever sanctified and given honour to manual labour. So becoming a Christian should make us better and more dependable workers and this would fulfil Paul's closing admonition on this topic – *"So that your daily life may win the respect of outsiders"* and *"so that you will not be dependent on anyone," 4:12.*

Paul instructed slaves to *"be subject to their masters in everything, to try to please them, not to talk back to them and not to steal from them, but to show that they can be fully trusted"*, and by doing this they would *"make the teaching about God our Saviour attractive,"* (Titus 2:9,10). Paul teaches us that our relationship with Christ should affect and impact every part of our lives – our life in the home, in Church and in the work place and such Christ-like conduct in each of these human spheres will bring honour to God and contribute to the advancing of the

Kingdom of God. What we believe is important but real belief will always be demonstrated by how we behave.

In 1 Thessalonians 4 Paul has given clear instruction on the kind of behaviour in daily life that will be pleasing to God – our behaviour in Church, in marriage and the home and at work. In 1 Thessalonians 5:12-20 he goes on to give instruction on the importance of right relationships as well as right behaviour. Our relationship with fellow believers is very important to God especially the relationship between the leaders and the members:

- *The relationship of the leaders to the people.* Paul underlines three responsibilities of leaders – to work (hard) at the task of leadership, to care for the flock and to admonish (close, personal instruction) when required.

- *The relationship of the people to the leaders.* There are two extremes to be avoided – of thinking too highly of leaders or demeaning them – putting them on a pedestal or in the pedal bin! Paul says that appreciation and affection are appropriate and good leaders are worthy of both because of the work they are doing. The end product of leaders leading well and people responding well will be a Church enjoying the fruit of peace and harmony.

- *The relationship of the people to each other.* The existence of good leaders doesn't absolve the people from a responsibility of care for each other. Three groups of people are highlighted for special attention – those who are unruly, they need to be warned; those who are timid, they need to be encouraged; those who are weak, they need to be helped. There are vulnerable people in every

Church and spiritual people will watch out for them and not 'write-them-off' but will do what is necessary to bring them back into health – *"always strive to do what is good for each other" (v15).*

- *The relationship of the people to God in worship – vs16-21.* In these few verses we get a taste of some aspects of what it would be like to meet in a healthy first century Church gathering. There would be joyful praise, continuous prayer, thanksgiving, operation of the gifts of the Spirit (not to be despised) – which would involve the singing of psalms, hymns and spiritual songs, giving testimonies, exercising the gifts of the Spirit and exhortations There was also the important place for the reading of the Scriptures – from v27 Paul gives a strong *("I charge you")* instruction to the leaders that they had to ensure that the Word was read to the people.

4. Paul's Prayers

Paul was an outstanding preacher of the gospel motivated by an unapologetic conviction that it was the power of God that saves. He also was an amazing Pastor, showing untiring care for his converts as well as giving relevant teaching for every sphere of their lives. He and the other leaders supplied the converts with living examples of how to live the Christian life. In addition, he knew how to pray for them.

Paul's intense pain at being separated from the new converts so soon after their conversion is seen in 1 Thessalonians 2:17-20. When it became so overpowering, he took the risk of sending Timothy back to the city to see how they were faring. Timothy's return with good news of their steadfastness fills him with an overwhelming joy which he expresses in heart-felt prayer. In his prayers for the Thessalonians (See 1 Thessalonians 1:2,3; 9-13; 5:23 and 2 Thessalonians 1:11,12; 2:13-17 and 3:16) as well as thanksgiving to God for answers, Paul prays for specific things that are relevant to the Thessalonian situation – they are model pastoral prayers:

- The removal of obstacles so that the apostles can return to Thessalonica
- Their love for each other to continue to grow
- Their faith to get stronger
- To stand firm for God
- The persecuted believers to be strengthened, to stand true and be found blameless at their Lord's return
- The new believers to live lives that are worthy of the Lord
- To know the peace of God in the midst of their trials

In the Thessalonian Church we have a wonderful combination of leaders with Holy Ghost authority and outstanding integrity joined with members who were fully committed to God and obedient to His Word. We see in this Church the three stages of the gospel in people's lives:

1. How the gospel came to them – *"our gospel came to you, not simply with words, but also with power..."* Paul reasoned, explained, proved and proclaimed Christ. He spoke with great confidence of Christ's death, resurrection and return. The disciples were well taught and pastored and had wonderful examples to follow in the lives of the three evangelists.

2. The reception they gave the gospel – *"you welcomed the message with the joy given by the Holy Spirit... you accepted it as the Word of God, which is indeed at work in you who believe"*, the harvest was abundant because the soil was so good.

3. How they shared the gospel – *"the Lord's message rang out from you, not only in Macedonia and Achaia – your faith in God has become known everywhere"*, the message of transformed lives 'thundered out' from Thessalonica.

Amazing converts, outstanding leaders, it's no wonder this Church attracted opposition – they were a serious threat to Satan. What was happening in the lives of these new converts was being talked about in the inns, bazaars and markets of the city. They had left their previous lives of idolatry, immorality and materialism and were now worshippers of the 'One True God'.

This transformed life-style was obvious in their marriage and home-life, in their sacrificial fellowship with fellow believers and in their work-life. The word was spreading beyond the city. It was all over Macedonia and Achaia. In fact the testimony of their changed lives was spreading everywhere but the cost was high. Paul speaks in 2 Corinthians 8 of their severe trials and extreme poverty but it was compensated by overflowing joy from the Holy Spirit.

Part 2

The Revelation of Jesus Christ

If I put on green-tinted glasses then everything I look at would be coloured green. The glasses would become a lens through which I would see the world. Paul wanted the Thessalonian converts to have a new lens through which they would interpret the world they lived in. Before conversion they had seen the world through the eyes of pagans whose lives were controlled by the weird worship of worthless idols. But now they were Christians, and when a believer comes to an understanding of the return of Jesus it should become a lens through which every aspect of life will be 'coloured'.

His return reminds us that life on earth is not forever and that what we do now will have a major impact in eternity. The lens of the truth of His return assures us that the difficulties of the present are temporary,

> *For our light and momentary troubles are achieving for us an eternal glory that far outweighs them all.*
>
> 2 Corinthians 4:17

The new life-style of the Thessalonians was a reflection of their belief in the expected return of the Lord – their growing and expanding faith, their abounding love for each other, their powerful, clear cut testimony, their overflowing joy from the Holy Spirit, their generous, sacrificial giving, and their fiery persecution. Your spiritual life will be richer for spending time with these first century believers; they will inspire you and help counteract the influence of the secularised Christianity which surrounds us today.

On the Island of Patmos the apostle John was given a revelation of final events which will certainly take place at a time in history known only to God. The future has been determined by God and will certainly come to pass exactly as He has decreed. God does not have a range of options that He will select from, depending on how things turn out. The final chapter of the world's history has already been written and will play out as He has determined. The writers of Scripture have recorded sufficient information for the people of God to be aware of what is happening and thus be able to *'live in the light of His coming'*. Special blessing is promised to those who will give diligent attention to the book of Revelation,

> *Blessed is the one who reads aloud the words of this prophecy, and blessed are those who hear it and take to heart what is written in it, because the time is near.*
>
> Revelation 1:3

Revelation is not an easy book to read but it is essential reading if you want to be living in readiness for our Lord's return.

Teaching on the return of Jesus is dealt with more in 1 and 2 Thessalonians than in any of Paul's other letters. It is mentioned in every chapter of the first letter with a total of 40 of the 138 verses given to this subject over the two letters. Along with Jesus' Olivet Discourse (Matthew 24 and 25) and the book of Revelation they supply us with significant knowledge for our understanding of the events surrounding the promised revelation of Jesus. His return is the next most important event for the people of our planet and, as I said earlier, at His return every person who is alive and all who have ever lived since the beginning of time, will stand before

God when the accurate record books of heaven will be opened on every life and each person will face God's judgment. None will escape.

For the worshippers of God there will also be judgment, not on their sin, but on their service. *Our redemption* is based on what *Christ has done*, our *rewards* are based on what *we have done* (Revelation 22:12). This will be a time for rewards and regrets – rewards for all that was done in His Name and regrets for what was not done but could have been. The time left between now and the Lord's return is an opportunity for unsaved people to respond to God's offer of salvation and that same time is an opportunity for every believer to use their time, energy and resources to advance His Kingdom, do His will and glorify His Name (read 1 Corinthians 3:10–15).

In Romans 13:11-14 Paul underlines the importance of us living our lives in the light of His coming,

> *And do this, understanding the present time: the hour has already come for you to wake up from your slumber, because our salvation is nearer now than when we first believed. The night is nearly over; the day is almost here. So let us put aside the deeds of darkness and put on the armour of light...clothe yourselves with the Lord Jesus Christ and do not think about how to gratify the desires of the flesh.*

The last recorded words of Jesus are in Revelation 22:20 – *"I am coming soon"* and the last prayer is from the lips of John, the last survivor of the twelve apostles – *"Amen, Come Lord Jesus"*. The Spirit, the whole Creation and the Church are all groaning, waiting for the transformation that will take place when our Lord returns.

Understanding and unpacking the events surrounding the return of the Lord can be complicated as there are different ways of interpretation. Also, it can be an unhelpful diversion to concentrate on working out the exact sequence of events and a chronological timetable of how things will happen.

As I have read through the Thessalonian letters my conclusion is that Paul's chief concern was that the converts would be motivated by their knowledge of Christ's return – motivated to a life of holiness, evangelism and security.

In Titus 2 Paul reminds us that the grace of God which introduced us to salvation also instructed us in how to behave as Christians,

> *"It teaches us to say 'no' to ungodliness and worldly passions and to live self-controlled, upright and godly lives in this present age..."*

Paul goes on to give the motivation for this transformed life-style,

> *"...**while we wait for the blessed hope** – the appearing of the glory of our great God and Saviour, Jesus Christ, who gave himself for us to redeem us from all wickedness and to purify for Himself a people that are his very own, eager to do what is good."*
>
> Titus 2:12–15

The anticipated and imminent return of our Lord therefore should be a strong incentive for us to live in constant readiness to stand before God at any moment.

Background to Paul's Second Coming Teaching in the Thessalonian letters

There was a local situation that compelled Paul to write so much in the Thessalonian Letters on the certainty of Christ's return. The malicious members of the circumcision group were at work spreading lies and false rumours about Paul and what he was teaching – especially his teaching on the Lord's return.

Paul wasn't completely sure of the source of this confusion but there was some teaching circulating, possibly by means of a spurious letter or a prophecy allegedly from Paul stating that the Day of the Lord had already happened (2 Thessalonians 2:1-3). What was being attributed to Paul was a contradiction of what he had already taught so Timothy reported that there was confusion and that this confusion was manifesting itself in three distinct issues:

- Confusion over what happened to believers who died before the Lord's return (1 Thessalonians 4:13-18)
- The misuse of Second Coming teaching to justify giving up work (2 Thessalonians 3:6-15)
- A mistaken belief that the Day of the Lord had already happened (2 Thessalonians 2:2)

Paul had previously given them teaching on these matters but it was obvious they needed further instruction and clarification because they were being *'unsettled and alarmed'* and that could lead to seeds of deception being sown in the young Church.

Before we try and unpack some of the events associated with our Lord's appearing and the finale of history, it might help to have some understanding of what happened at the very beginning.

Satan, the Arch Rebel

At the heart of all rebellion and wickedness is Satan, the one-time angel of light who became the prince of darkness.

Satan is not a myth, he is not a joke and he is not an ugly creature with horns, a forked tail and carrying a pitch-fork. We would be surprised how beautiful and dazzling he could appear – yes, as a roaring lion but also like an angel of light. He has not always been around. There was a moment when he was created which is described in Ezekiel 28:11-19. Initially this chapter is a prophecy about an earthly king of Tyre but the progress of the language used takes the prophecy beyond the description of an earthly king into the realm of a non-human being.

The creation of Lucifer

At a point in eternity, before earthly time began, God decided to create a new angelic being. It is obvious that Ezekiel (the writer) was conscious of the limitation of human language needed to describe this creation of God – dazzling in beauty and unequalled in intelligence. No human beings had as yet been created so Ezekiel was receiving prophetic insight from God about this moment in eternity so that he could record the event for others to know about it.

The words given by the Holy Spirit are factual not hyperbole, and they leave us with a sense of amazement at the description of this new angel – *"the model of perfection, full of wisdom and perfect in beauty....every precious stone adorned you: ruby, topaz and emerald, chrysolite, onyx and jasper, sapphire, turquoise and beryl. Your settings and mountings were made of gold."*

The passage in Ezekiel 28 goes on to describe the exalted and privileged position that this newly created angel enjoyed – *"You were anointed as a guardian cherub, for so I ordained you"*.

This beautiful creation was with God on the Holy mountain of God, among the fiery stones and was with God in Eden. The name given to this new being was *Lucifer* which means 'brightness, morning star, bright star' and in Isaiah 14:12 he was called *'morning star, son of the dawn'*. Lucifer was ahead of all the other angels in beauty and intelligence and in closeness to God. He was a guardian cherub responsible for the protection of the throne of God and in the closest, most intimate proximity to God.

Despite his beauty, his wisdom, his privileged position and his anointed ministry, he rebelled by stepping beyond the bounds laid down by God and became the leader of a wider rebellion among the angels. This resulted in a third of their number being infected by his deception and finally cast out of heaven along with him. His expulsion was a public humiliation for Satan and birthed in him a deep-seated and eternal hatred for God that would stop at nothing to hurt God, especially if it involved God's family.

The rebellion of Lucifer

How could such a beautiful, dazzling and perfect creation of God become the implacable enemy of God that we now know as Satan – from an angel of light to the prince of darkness? Time, as we know it, did not yet exist, so we have no idea how long it was after his creation that Lucifer changed. Did he see a reflection of himself somewhere and suddenly become impressed with his dazzling beauty? How it happened is not as important as the fact that Lucifer had the power to make a choice and he made a disastrous one that had long term repercussions for the whole of creation.

In Isaiah 14 in the record of the widespread devastation caused to many nations by the violence of the Babylonians we see a reflection of the havoc caused by Satan to all nations, but the decisive end to Belshazzar and the Babylonians at the hands of Darius (see Daniel 5) is a foreshadowing of the ultimate judgment that will fall on Satan when he meets his final end by the hand of God (Revelation 20:7-10).

It is important for us to understand the nature of Lucifer's original sin because it will give us an insight into the nature of his final sin and judgment. The Bible describes the basis of his rebellion against God in Isaiah 14:12-14. Once again, as in Ezekiel, the context of the prophecy is about an earthly king but the language quite obviously goes beyond the description of a human ruler.

Behind the evil rulers referred to by Isaiah and Ezekiel there is the controlling influence of an angelic non-human being. This passage records the five pride-based motives that controlled Lucifer's bid to usurp the authority of God. The ambitions of Lucifer are audaciously repugnant. In Ezekiel 28:15 God says, *'Wickedness was found in you'*. Isaiah is more specific in describing this 'wickedness'. His wickedness was all rooted in pride,

> *"**I will** ascend to heaven, **I will** raise my throne above the stars (angels) of God, **I will** sit enthroned on the mount of assembly, on the utmost heights of the sacred mountain, **I will** ascend above the tops of the clouds, **I will** make myself like the most high."*

God declared of Lucifer,

> *"Your heart became proud on account of your beauty and you corrupted your wisdom because of your splendour."*
>
> Ezekiel 28:17

Verse 16 of the same passage informs us, *'Through your widespread trade you were filled with violence'*. To trade is to offer something of benefit in exchange for something else. Is this referring to Lucifer 'trading' with the rebellious angels, offering what he could not give in exchange for their participation in his violent rebellion against God and the righteous angels? (2 Peter 2:4). Lucifer wanted to take over heaven. He wanted to be served, not to serve, he wanted to be God and be worshipped not be a worshipper and he tried to do secret deals with the angels to fulfil his ambition. His ambition to replace God resulted in war in heaven with heaven's army being led by Michael the arch angel. Michael and the angels triumphed and Satan, along with the rebellious angels, was cast out of heaven, (Revelation 12).

Behind wicked, earthly kings and rulers (like the King of Tyre and Babylon referred to in Ezekiel and Isaiah) who display this same pride and arrogance, lurks the control of Lucifer (Satan) who still has ambitions to usurp God. Behind wicked earthly rulers is the power of *'rulers, authorities, powers of this dark world, spiritual forces of evil in the heavenly realms'* (Ephesians 6:12).

They are at war with God and His Kingdom but the conflict is moving towards the pre-determined climax when Lucifer, who is now Satan, will receive his final judgment after he has, for the last time, deceived the nations. The closing chapters of Revelation declare that God will command a strong angel to bind him and cast him into a place of eternal judgment along with the beast and the false prophet (Revelation 20:7-10) never again to be the tempter.

The expulsion of Satan from heaven

Lucifer's violent rebellion against God was met with an immediate and decisive response from God. It was as fast as lightning and all the inhabitants of heaven witnessed it (Luke 10:18). When his wickedness was uncovered Ezekiel 28 and Isaiah 14 record God's response,

> *"I drove you in disgrace from the mount of God, I expelled you O guardian cherub...I threw you to the earth, I made a spectacle of you before kings...All the nations who knew you are appalled at you...you have come to a horrible end...you are brought down to the grave, to the depths of the pit."*

Satan was tempted by his pride and paid the price when he was expelled from his exalted position close to the throne of God. Pride in any shape or form is abhorrent to God. 1 Peter 5:5 tells us that God opposes the proud; He is at war with pride because it started sin in the universe with all the devastating results that have ensued.

Satan – the evil tempter

The expulsion of Satan from heaven and his relegation to earth was a public humiliation for him. As a result, he has an extreme hatred for God and will do anything to vent his anger at the Almighty. One way he does this is by temptation, by which he subtly or blatantly attempts to lure people away from obedience to God. Before the creation, he had successfully tempted a large number of angels by offering an allegedly better deal with *him* on the throne rather than *God.* The angels very quickly learned that his promises were hollow and carried an awful price – expulsion from the light and joy of God's presence to the darkness and misery of Satan's domain where they are held in chains of darkness awaiting their final judgment and relegation to the abyss (Jude v6 and 2 Peter 2:4).

The next example of Satan at work as the tempter is found in Genesis when Satan tempted Eve to disobey the one, simple command that God had given to her and her husband. The temptation of Adam and Eve is recorded for us in some detail in Genesis 3 because it has a lot to teach us about how temptation works. Temptation is an unwelcome part of living in a fallen world. Satan is referred to as,

> *The god of this age who has blinded the minds of unbelievers so that they cannot see the light of the gospel of the glory of Christ, who is the image of God.*
>
> 2 Corinthians 4:4

Satan's constant work is to stop people discovering and accepting God's offer of eternal salvation through Jesus Christ and for those who have received Christ into their lives, his work is to drive a wedge between the believer and Christ by tempting them to disobey God's commands. The most audacious attempt at temptation by Satan was when he tried to tempt our Lord in the wilderness where again we see Satan's naked ambition for deity when he offered Jesus all the kingdoms of this world if He would fall down and worship him.

Know your enemy

In any warfare, intelligence is essential for victory. To know your enemy, his tactics, resources, plans, strengths and weaknesses will give any army an advantage to secure victory over an enemy.

Intelligence played a big part in Israel's victory in the Six-Day War of 1967. The Jewish nation was surrounded on all sides by several very hostile Arab nations who were determined to eliminate them, and with combined forces that were greater than Israel's it seemed a foregone conclusion that they would lose. Israel faced a combined force that had a two-to-one advantage in manpower, two-to-one in tanks, seven-to-one in artillery, three-to-one in aircraft and four-to-one in warships and not only were the opposing nations greater in manpower and equipment, the equipment was also superior and more advanced. It seemed a one-sided conflict with an inevitable outcome. However, because of detailed intelligence, Israel was able, in the first hour of the first day of the war to destroy or disable the majority of Egypt's air force and runways. They knew the location of every Egyptian squadron and the lay-out of every air-base and this air strike immediately gave them air superiority.

This pre-emptive strike, based on meticulous intelligence under the command of Aaron Yariv was crucial to the final decisive victory. His insistence to 'know-your-enemy' proved its worth in the short six-day war. In the two years before the war Yariv made it his business to know every detail of the enemy's capabilities and movements. His insistence to 'know-your-enemy' certainly proved its worth.

While the Christian must not make Satan the focus of attention, they must know their enemy and his tactics. The Bible is an accurate, dependable and sufficient source of information for us to know our foe. The Apostle Paul declared, *'We are not ignorant of his devices'* (2 Corinthians 2:11). Sadly, however, too many Christians are ignorant of Satan's schemes and tactics and are therefore caught out too easily. We have sufficient intelligence for us to know his schemes and his tactics so we need never be caught out or put at a disadvantage.

But as well as knowing our enemy, we must also know the resources that God has provided for us which are totally sufficient for every believer to be an overcomer and victor in this conflict. The Word of God is the sword of the Spirit and the offensive weapon in the Christian's armour. We have a victorious Commander, the right weapons to be victorious and we also have the added advantage of the angelic armies of heaven. Billy Graham referred to them as 'God's secret agents'; they are commissioned by God to be our constant allies in this spiritual warfare.

This titanic struggle is very real; it is not a game or just an interesting topic for debate. The final outcome will eclipse everything else in history; it has eternal consequences and will determine the future of the whole of creation. It will also involve every single person on the planet. Every believer will be a focus for the vicious, unrelenting onslaughts of Satan or, if not a follower of Christ, then a part of Satan's rebellion against God. The final conflict will divide humanity into two very clear-cut opposing forces. There will be no place for neutrality or conscientious abstention, and people will be either on the side of Christ or part of the opposition. This final conflict will be the culmination of the age-long battle between God and Satan – and Satan loses!

We have already looked at Jesus' warning in Matthew 24 where He told His disciples that Satan's opposition in the days approaching His return would be ruthless. He warned that many nominal Christians would be caught out by deception; many would turn away from the faith because of persecution and because of the escalating presence of wickedness the love of many would grow cold – persecution, wickedness and deception – Satan's three-pronged assault on believers. This is a serious and solemn warning from the mouth of Jesus that needs to receive the maximum attention of every believer but sadly, especially in the decadent Western hemisphere where too many Christians are sleep-walking into the final conflict, they will be casualties, not conquerors, in the end-time battle.

When Jude sat down to write his letter, he had in mind the subject of the salvation that all believers share in. However, as he thought about the situation the Church of his day was facing he changed his mind and declared,

> *I found it necessary to write to you exhorting you to contend earnestly for the faith which was once for all delivered to the saints.*
>
> Jude v3

Jude felt compelled to write this in the first century, I wonder what he would say about Christian life in the twenty first century. Jude went on to say that,

> *Certain men have crept in unnoticed, who long ago were marked out for this condemnation, ungodly men, who turn the grace of our God into lewdness and deny the only Lord God and our Lord Jesus Christ.*
>
> Jude v4

The Christian Church today is under major assault from ungodly people who are substituting the culture of the day for biblical truth, and many are being deluded by attractive heresies that may be popular with the world but are anathema to the Spirit of Truth. This is a day for all Spirit-filled believers to earnestly contend for the unalterable faith that has been given to us in God's Word.

We must reject the slackness and carelessness that is engulfing many believers in the affluent West. Church attendance is optional and intermittent – attending one service every three weeks has become normal for many, personal Bible reading and prayer is sporadic and holiness is a foreign concept with standards of conduct that leave the Christian as hardly distinguishable from a non-Christian. We are seeing a fulfilling of the prophecy of Jesus – many departing from the faith, many deceived and the love of most growing cold (see also 1 Thessalonians 5:4-11).

The Day of the Lord

Please read 2 Thessalonians 2:1-12.

Because of the relentless undermining efforts of the Judaisers by means of a forged letter or a garbled account of a spurious prophecy allegedly from Paul, some of the members of the Thessalonica Church thought that the Day of the Lord had occurred and so they had somehow 'missed out'. This left them confused.

The Christian's hope for the future is centred on Jesus and His promised return to finish the work He started at the cross. The death and resurrection of Jesus is the vital basis for confidence that He will certainly return and complete the work of salvation for all believers,

> *For we believe that Jesus died and rose again, and so we believe that God will bring with Jesus those who have fallen asleep in Him.*
>
> 1 Thessalonians 4:14

As sure as we believe that the first statement is true (that Jesus rose from the grave) so we can confidently believe that the second statement will be fulfilled (that Jesus will come again). This is the Christian's hope for the future. The hope of His coming is the lens through which we view all of life and the way we see the future will have a profound effect on how we live in the present – people who lose hope for the future face depression and despair.

The pagan world that the Thessalonian converts lived in was devoid of hope, much like the depressed state of society today, but the Christian's hope is a confident expectation of a glorious eternal future with God in heaven so it is vital for every believer to have a clear understanding of the Scripture's teaching on this important subject and thus have a sure, dependable foundation for their future in the midst of turbulent end-time events.

The Christian hope is sure and certain but that does not detract from the fact that the final conflict, prior to His triumphant appearing, will be ferocious,

> *If those days had not been cut short no one would survive, but for the sake of the elect those days will be shortened.*
>
> Matthew 24:22

The second chapter of 2 Thessalonians is an important one but also a 'difficult-to-interpret' one. Paul writes to assure the Thessalonians that they had not missed out on the coming of Jesus. He writes so that they will not be 'unsettled' – disturbed in their thinking or 'alarmed' – in a state of anxiety. If both of these conditions were allowed to continue it could lead to their being deceived.

Paul declares that the Day of the Lord cannot yet have happened because two events must take place before that

'Day' arrives. These events are the outbreak of the rebellion and the arrival of the man of lawlessness (The Antichrist); the advent of the rebel and the rebellion.

The 'Day of the Lord' introduces a big subject. It is also referred to as 'The Day', 'The Day of the Lord Jesus Christ', 'The Day of Jesus Christ', 'that Day' etc. It refers to God's final reckoning with a rebellious creation and it is spoken of throughout the Old Testament and the New Testament. It will be God's flaming Day of Judgment on all His enemies, His day of vindication and victory over every opposition and the total end to all that has blighted our world since the Fall in Eden – sickness, evil, disease, death, war, hatred, Satan and all his angels and the grave will be emptied, never to be filled again. In every respect, this 'Day' is about Jesus Christ, it is His Day. It will be a time of unimaginable terror for this Christ rejecting world but a time of overflowing joy for God's people.

Paul gives his revelation on three important matters preceding the appearing of Jesus – the arrival of The Antichrist, the final rebellion against God and the perpetration of 'the lie'. We will make a brief examination of these three precursors to the appearing of Christ.

(1) The Man Of Lawlessness

We have learned earlier of Satan's beginning, his beauty and intelligence but also his wickedness and rebellion which resulted in his being expelled from heaven. However, as the world now accelerates towards final judgment, we see that Satan's expulsion from heaven has not changed his original ambition – he is just as wicked and lawless and through the person of his tool, The Antichrist, he will once again make his bid (his final bid) to replace God on the throne of heaven.

Antichrist is a human being who will be manifest at a pre-ordained time when the world will be staggering under the load of insurmountable problems, and he will have the appearance of a man of peace who has answers for the mounting problems that are overwhelming humanity. The Antichrist will be a tool of Satan and despite the initial appearance of being a man of peace, he will prove to be the embodiment of all that is cruel, evil and destructive, and he will have as his main target, the people of God, Jewish and Church.

History has seen many that are forerunners of the end-time dictator. One example is Hitler who came to power and prominence at a time when the German nation was struggling to recover from the effects and cost of World War I. He came to power on a tide of popular euphoria at his ability to solve the nation's problems, but once he had established his power base his true ambitions began to emerge and many German people began to realise that they had a monster in the seat of power. From 2 Thessalonians 2 we learn that this *'man of lawlessness and wickedness'* will set himself up in opposition to everything to do with God. In fact, he will set himself up as God and demand to be worshipped as God, very much like some of the Roman Caesars who demanded that Christians had to declare – 'Caesar is Lord' which, of course, they would not do and so died in their tens of thousands.

Down the centuries many names have been put forward as The Antichrist – some secular and some religious: Antiochus Epiphanes, Muhammad, the Papacy, Napoleon, Hitler, and Stalin etc. In chapter 2 of Thessalonians, Paul goes on to explain that when Antichrist appears he will have superhuman power,

> *The coming of the lawless one will be in accordance with how Satan works. He will use all*

> *sorts of displays of power through signs and wonders that serve the lie, and all the ways that wickedness deceives those who are perishing.*
>
> 2 Thessalonians 2:9,10

Daniel had a vision of the coming of this man of wickedness and describes him as,

> *"as a master of intrigue...he will become very strong but not by his own power....he will cause deceit to prosper and he will consider himself superior."*
>
> Daniel 8:23-25

The power of Antichrist is already at work in the world but 'restrained' until it is God's time for him to be fully revealed. His revealing (uncovering) to the world is spoken of three times in chapter two of 2 Thessalonians (vs 3, 6 and 8) and will precede the revealing of Jesus Christ but it will not take place until *"the proper time"* – God's pre-ordained time.

Revelation 13 gives some further clues to the character of The Antichrist. He will be given great authority by Satan and despite an attempt to kill him, the wound will be healed and coupled with his display of counterfeit miracles, the whole world will be filled with wonderment at his dazzling display of power. He will have a 42 month long, intense reign and will have temporary victory in his war against the people of God – the only ones who withstand him and who have refused to have the mark of the Antichrist applied to their right hand or forehead. By refusing his mark, God's people (Jews and Christians) will knowingly and deliberately open themselves up to the vicious hatred of Satan. The Bible declares that this time of savagery will be unlike anything that history has ever recorded,

> *For then there will be great distress, unequalled from the beginning of the world until now – and never to be equalled again.*
>
> Matthew 24:21

> *He will speak against the Most High and oppress His holy people and try to change the set times and the laws. The holy people will be delivered into his hands for a time, times and half a time (42 months).*
>
> Daniel 7:25

But this will be the prelude to his end,

> *The court will sit, and his power will be taken away and completely destroyed forever. Then the sovereignty, power and greatness of all the kingdoms under heaven will be handed over to the holy people of the Most High. His kingdom will be an everlasting kingdom, and all rulers will worship and obey Him.*
>
> Daniel 7:26, 27

The Restrainer

Paul had obviously given verbal instruction to the Thessalonians on the subject of the Antichrist (as had also the Apostle John),

> *Don't you remember that when I was with you I used to tell you these things. And now you know what is holding him back, so that he will be revealed at the proper time. For the secret power of lawlessness is already at work; but the one who holds it back will continue to do so until he is taken*

out of the way. And then the lawless one will be revealed.

2 Thessalonians 2:5-8

On the basis of what Paul had taught them, it is obvious that the Thessalonians would understand what he was referring to when he said, *"And now you know what is holding him back so that he may be revealed at the proper time" (v6).* We don't have the benefit of their insight so we have to come to the best conclusion we can on the identity of 'the restrainer'. From these verses in 2 Thessalonians 2 we are told that there are two forces working simultaneously in our world:

1. The first one is subversive, masterminded by Satan in his persistent determination to hurt God and his creation. It is called *"the power of lawlessness"* and is dedicated to the overthrow of all law, order and decency but especially the law of God or anything associated with God. This spirit of lawlessness has been operating in our world ever since Satan (then Lucifer) led his abortive attempt to take over the throne of God. It is progressively working towards the final conflict between good and evil.

2. Counteracting the power of lawlessness is another force acting as a resistance that is hindering the full onslaught of lawlessness. As long as this counteracting force is operational, lawlessness is unable to fully manifest itself. But these verses in 2 Thessalonians 2 tell us that God has ordained a time *("the proper time")* when this 'restraining' force will be removed and so will commence the sequence of events that will lead up to the revealing of Jesus Christ in all of His might and glory with the final solution to the ages-long war of Satan's war against the authority of God.

We look now at the question of 'who or what is the restrainer'? This restraining influence has been in operation down the ages but its day of removal is getting closer. That will signal the unleashing of the full fury of Satan's fearsome hatred against God which will be the short prelude to the appearing of Jesus. The interpretation of who or what the restrainer is has created a lot of speculation; some see the answer to be the power of the Holy Spirit at work through the Church and others the restraining influence of the State or Government. My personal conclusion is the State or good Government. In the early years of the 1st century Church there were times when the apostles benefited from the protection of the State against the vicious attacks of Judaism.

There are several essential pillars that support a civilised society and hold it together – vital institutions that are critical for stability in a functioning group. There are the pillars of the Family, Religion, Law and Justice, Government and Education. Instability in any one of these 'pillars' will have a knock-on, detrimental effect on the others. Effective Government is good men joining together to keep bad men in check. Civilised Government exists to defend freedom with force, if necessary, and so will pass and enforce laws that allow citizens to go about their daily business (including worship) in peace and it will defend the weak and the vulnerable. A peaceful society knows the benefit of good laws so it is not hard therefore to see civilised government as 'the restrainer' working to keep lawlessness at bay. However, as we look out on our own society we are aware of powerful forces that are seeking to undermine the rule of law and when the day dawns for the collapse of the rule of law and order, mankind will feel the tsunami of Satan's final attempt to establish his authority on a deceived world.

When the time comes for Satan's 'appearing' he will not, at first, be perceived as a man of lawlessness. In fact, in all probability he will appear as the exact opposite – a convincing, peace-loving leader who will understand the complexity of the international problems and more importantly, he will appear to have solutions. Such will be the desperation of world leaders at that time for solutions that in a very short period of time, total power will be handed over to The Antichrist and his grip on earthly sovereignty will be complete. This will allow him to uncover his true intentions.

There are examples, currently and in history, of bad government and the people languishing under its yoke are the first to rejoice at its removal, but even bad government is better than the chaos of no government. Scriptures teach Christians to support government in society, even when the administration is less than perfect,

> *Let everyone be subject to the governing authorities, for there is no authority except that which God has established. The authorities that exist have been established by God. Consequently, whoever rebels against the authority is rebelling against what God has instituted, and those and those who do so will bring judgment on themselves. For rulers hold no terror for those who do right, but for those who do wrong...They are God's servants, agents of wrath to bring punishment on the wrongdoer. Therefore it is necessary to submit to the authorities, not only because of possible punishment but also as a matter of conscience.*
>
> *Romans 13:1-10 (See also 1 Peter 2:11-21)*

Behind good, well-ordered government and a well-run society, is the plan and purpose of God but on the dark side, behind state oppression, injustice, cruelty and corruption is the destructive power of Satan whose motivation is to rob, kill and destroy.

Before we move on to the subject of 'The Rebellion' it is good to remind ourselves that Antichrist's reign of terror will, mercifully, be shortened by God (see Matthew 24:22) and his fate has already been determined – he is the man,

> *Doomed to destruction...whom the Lord Jesus will overthrow with the breath of his mouth and destroy by the splendour of his coming.*
>
> 2 Thessalonians 2:3,8

We have looked at The Rebel, now we will look at 'The Rebellion'.

(2) The Rebellion

The three major events – the final Rebellion, the appearance of The Antichrist and the launch of the biggest Lie, are all closely linked. Once The Antichrist makes his appearance, the Rebellion will very quickly follow and during this Rebellion the Lie will be presented.

Ever since Lucifer, the angel of light, rebelled against the order of heaven, there has been rebellion in God's creation and this rebellion will reach a crescendo when Satan, the arch rebel, will lead the final rebellion during the Tribulation. Rebellion against God is Satan's basic character just as obedience is part of Christ's basic character. When created he was 'the angel of light' but then, because of his pride, he became 'the prince of darkness'. Satan cannot touch God so he directs his fury against the family of God – Jewish and Christian.

Shortly after the Genesis creation, Satan infected the whole human race with the venom of his rebellion by tempting Adam and Eve in the Garden of Eden. He lied to them and promised what he could not deliver and they were taken in by his deception. Because Satan is the one behind this final rebellion, it will chiefly be against the laws of God but it will result in a breakdown of all law and order leading to unprecedented chaos.

We can already see the systematic and progressive move of society away from God's laws and the determined attempts to remove all Christian influence from society – *'the secret power of lawlessness is already at work'*. Through the destruction of all law and order the Antichrist will *'oppose and exalt himself over everything that is called God or is worshipped'*. This will be the forerunner of Satan, in the person of his tool, the Antichrist, who will *'set himself up in God's Temple, proclaiming himself to be God (the Lie)'*. The stage is being set for the final confrontation and the restraining force of civilised government is gradually being eroded in preparation for this final open rebellion. This will be a time of unrestrained social and moral chaos when all that is good, decent and just will be swept aside by Satan's final attempt to overthrow all the stability of God's order.

What a totally horrific nightmare scenario – a society where all law and order has broken down. The war between God and Satan is escalating from the covert power of lawlessness at work attempting to destabilise society held in check from open rebellion by 'the restrainer', to the blatant and undisguised rebellion of Satan's short reign.

Today's world wants freedom with no restraints, the freedom to make up its own moral standards and to decide how they will run their lives. Well, society will get what it wants (briefly) but the price will be unimaginable. Listen to Paul's description of a society that has rebelled against God and biblical morality and where all restraints have been removed and swept away by a tide of moral wickedness,

> *But mark this: there will be terrible times in the last days. People will be lovers of themselves, lovers of money, boastful proud, abusive, disobedient to their parents, ungrateful, unholy, without love, unforgiving, slanderous, without self-control, brutal, not lovers of the good, treacherous, rash, conceited, lovers of pleasure rather than lovers of God – having a form of godliness but denying the power.*
>
> 2 Timothy 3:1-5

The appearing of Christ is getting ever closer but it will be preceded by the appearing of the Antichrist and though Antichrist's appearing will be accompanied by *"all sorts of displays of power through signs and wonders that serve the lie"* the appearing of Christ will have an immediate effect on him – *"whom the Lord Jesus will overthrow with the breath of his mouth and destroy with the splendour of his coming"*.

During the seven year period of time referred to as 'The Tribulation' when The Rebellion will occur, two opposing purposes will be in operation:

1. The time of God's wrath against sin – His pent-up anger against a rebellious and disobedient world
2. The time of Satan's wrath against God, directed at His people (the Jews) and His Church (Christians)

The time of God's wrath

Just a few days before going to His death, Jesus took time to give His disciples His most detailed teaching of what it will be like in the days immediately preceding His return. It is recorded in Matthew 24, Mark 13 and Luke 21 and is referred to as *'The Olivet Discourse'*. He compared this coming period to the Days of Noah and the Days of Lot. The Days of Noah, Genesis 6:5,6 and 11-13, describes the moral climate,

> *The Lord saw how great the wickedness of the human race had become on the earth and that every inclination of the thoughts of the human heart was only evil all the time. The Lord regretted that he had made human beings on the earth and his heart was deeply troubled...Now the earth was corrupt in God's sight and was full of violence. God saw how corrupt the earth had become, for all the people on earth had corrupted their ways..."for the earth is filled with violence because of them. I am going to destroy both them and the earth".*

Wickedness and violence were so rampant that God had no option but to destroy mankind and start again with Noah and his family.

Jesus also likened the coming period to the Days of Lot when sexual sin had reached a depth of depravity that, once again, God had no option but to step in and destroy the cities of Sodom and Gomorrah where the sin of homosexuality wasn't just wide spread, it was applauded and approved of by all of society and Noah was severely attacked because he dared to disagree with them (see Genesis 19). Certainly there were other sins in Sodom and Gomorrah – arrogant, overfed and unconcerned, they did not help the poor and the needy, they were haughty and did detestable things in God's sight (Ezekiel 16:49,50) but the sin of homosexuality attracted Divine judgment because it undermines and defiles a major part of our basic identity given to us by the Creator.

God is patient and merciful, desiring that all mankind repent and find salvation,

> *The Lord is not slow in keeping his promise (judgment), as some understand slowness. Instead He is patient with you, not wanting anyone to perish, but everyone to come to repentance.*
>
> 2 Peter 3:9

But there comes a point when the patience of God is exhausted. In the days of Noah, God waited for that long period of time while the Ark was being built but finally the flood of judgment came and God shut the door of the Ark. In the days of Lot, God would have spared the cities if He had been able to find ten righteous people and even sent two angels for a final attempt at changing their ways but to no avail. Lot and his family had to hurriedly leave before judgment fell.

In the generation that we are now living in, we see the acceleration of sin on every front, building up to that moment when God will say, "Enough" and so will begin the judgments and the wrath of God that the book of Revelation outlines for us.

This time of the terrifying wrath of God will come in three parts introduced by seven seals, seven trumpets and seven bowls, each growing in intensity and terror. People will know that what is coming on the earth is the judgment of God,

> *For the great day of his wrath has come and who can withstand it.*
>
> Revelation 6:17

Such will be the terror of the experience that they will call on the mountains and rocks to cover them and hide them from God's anger but astonishingly, despite the terror of the experience, people will refuse to repent of their sin,

The rest of mankind who were not killed by these plagues still did not repent of the work of their hands…nor did they repent of their murders, their magic arts, their sexual immorality or their thefts.

Revelation 9:20,21

This unbelievable response is repeated twice again in Revelation 16:9,11 and Revelation 14:6,7 records that God will even send a mighty angel on a mission of opportunity for all of mankind,

"Then I saw another angel flying in mid-air, and he had the eternal gospel to proclaim to those who live on the earth – to every nation, tribe, language and people. He said in a loud voice, 'Fear God and give Him glory, because the hour of His judgment has come. Worship Him who made the heavens, the earth, the sea and the springs of water".

Mercy in the midst of judgment – no one will ever be able to accuse God of not caring or not having patience.

John in his writing of the Book of Revelation was faced with the problem of finding language to fully express this time of cataclysmic events. Jesus described these coming days,

"For then there will be great distress, unequalled from the beginning of the world until now – and never to be equalled again. If those days had not been cut short, no one would survive, but for the sake of the elect those days will be shortened."

Matthew 24: 21, 22

In the midst of this time of divine judgment on an unrepentant world, the people of God will hear the heavenly summons to meet their Lord in the air and what will be a time of unimaginable joy for God's people will be a time of unimaginable mourning for the people of the world,

> *Then will appear the sign of the Son of Man in heaven. And then all the people of the earth shall mourn when they see the Son of Man coming on the clouds of heaven with power and great glory. And he will send his angels with a loud trumpet call and they will gather his elect from the four winds, from one end of heaven to the other.*
>
> Matthew 24:30, 31

See also 1 Thessalonians 4:16-18 for Paul's revelation of the intensely joyful period for Christ's Church.

John Stott's commentary *The Bible Speaks Today* has a helpful outline of this longed-for experience – the ***return*** of Christ for His Church, followed by the ***resurrection*** of the dead in Christ. Then the ***rapture*** will take place when those who are alive at that time will be caught up together with the resurrected dead in Christ to meet the Lord in the air. All of this will climax in the great ***reunion*** of all the saints of all the ages with the Lord never again to be parted from Him – *'encourage one another with these words'.*

The 'rapture' of God's Church will trigger the final and most intense period of the Tribulation which will witness the finale of the justified anger of God on an unrepentant and rebellious world – the outpouring of the seven bowls of God's wrath (Revelation 16).

During this highly intense period the people who have surrendered to the Antichrist and received his mark will come under God's fierce judgment and those who have refused and carry the seal of God on their forehead will come under the wrath of Satan (until the rapture).

The time of Satan's anger

In the first part of the Tribulation, when the Church is still on earth, and before the rapture, the hatred that Satan has for God will explode with ferocity on the people of God, Jewish and Christian. During this period those who receive the mark of the Beast will have access to all the necessities of life, but those who refuse will face unbelievable difficulties and persecution. When Jesus spoke of this period (see Matthew 24:10-12) He made it clear that there would be three major attacks on the followers of Christ – deception, wickedness and persecution – and because of the intensity of these attacks many Christians will be deceived, many will abandon the faith and most will see their love for Christ grow cold.

Refusal to accept the mark of the beast will result in severe suffering for disciples of Christ and many nominal Christians will surrender their faith for the sake of self-preservation. The outbreak of the fires of persecution is not the best time to be strengthening our walk with God. Our steadfast commitment to Christ and our walk with Him needs to be rooted and established now, before the storm breaks. If we will walk with Him in the easier times, He will walk with us in the hard times. Peter deluded himself about how strong he was before Christ was arrested but his eventual denial of Christ in front of a servant girl would always be a personal grief.

- The attack of ***persecution.*** Since the beginning of time there has been persecution of the righteous, from Cain's hatred and murder of his brother Abel up to the present time when more Christians are being martyred for Christ now than at any other time in history. There have been times when the Church has almost been wiped out but the persecution of the Tribulation period is in a totally different league. Such will be the ferocity of Satan's last onslaught on Christians that Jesus said that the period will be shortened to preserve life,

> *For then there will be great distress, unequalled from the beginning of the world until now – and never to be equalled again.*
>
> *(Matthew 24:21).*

- The attack of ***deception***. The most repeated warning in the New Testament is *'watch'*. It is so easy to neglect our spiritual lives. In His *Olivet Discourse* Jesus gives very pointed teaching on the path of persecution that will lie ahead for His disciples throughout the coming ages, but especially for those who will be alive in the days immediately preceding His return.

  In Mark's account of His discourse (chapter 13) Jesus warns seven times of the need for vigilance – *'watch, watch out, be on your guard (three times), be alert, keep watch'*. There was a very serious reason for this – the presence and the power of deception through Satan, the master and father of lies. He deceived a large number of the angels in his rebellion against God when he was Lucifer, the angel of light. He deceived Adam and Eve with his lies and false promises and down the ages he has had too much success in his disguise as an angel of light.

  Deception will be rampant in the Tribulation. Jesus predicted that false prophets and false gospels would abound in the final days of mankind's history – *"many false prophets will appear and deceive many people"* (Matthew 24:11). Paul further explains that the lying wonders of Satan will deceive those who have rejected the truth,

> *"They perish because they refused to love the truth and be saved. For this reason God sends them a powerful delusion so that they will believe the lie and so that all will be condemned who have not believed the truth but have delighted in wickedness."*
>
> 2 Thessalonians 2:10,11

When a person refuses to accept the truth, they are then open to be deceived by the lie.

- The attack of ***wickedness.*** This is a deliberate challenging and flouting of the laws of God. Since the beginning of time this work of Satan has been with us but in the days immediately preceding the appearing of Christ, wickedness will plumb the depths of depravity and just as Lot was *"distressed by the depraved conduct of the lawless (wicked) – for that righteous man living among them day after day was tormented in his righteous soul by the lawless deeds he saw and heard" (2 Peter 2:7,8)*, so believers alive at this time of the Tribulation will be assaulted by the blatant wickedness of that generation.

Under the rule of the Antichrist wickedness will be unrestrained which will result in the disappearance of all that is good, just and decent. Isaiah warned of these coming days,

> *Woe to those who call evil good and good evil, who put darkness for light and light for darkness.*
>
> Isaiah 5:20

We are already seeing the forward march of this secret (covert) power of lawlessness in preparation for the public unveiling of the man of wickedness (The Antichrist). Moral laws that have protected standards of decency and goodness for generations are being removed or rewritten by pressure from militant groups like LGBT, all in the name of inclusion and diversity. This last generation will take pleasure in wickedness and sadly, many nominal Christians will capitulate to this intolerant Political Correctness, motivated by the fear of being accused of bigotry or hate crimes.

It is probable that accepting the mark of the beast will carry with it acceptance of the perverted code of belief and conduct dictated by Antichrist's administration. The emerging of these days of the increase of wickedness will mean a crisis of choice for nominal believers, Jesus foretold that the love of most of these cool Christians will grow cold and they will leave the faith in order to gain temporary protection from the cost of carrying the mark of Christ. But Jesus adds at the end of his teaching,

> *"But the one who stands firm to the end will be saved."*
>
> Matthew 24:13

(3) The Lie

During the dark days of the Tribulation, when The Antichrist rules, those who 'delight in wickedness' and 'refuse to love or believe the truth' will be ensnared by Satan's greatest deception – *"For this reason God sends them a powerful delusion so that they will believe* ***the lie.****"* This is not a little white lie. In fact, it will be the most blatant and blackest lie ever imposed on humanity and astonishingly, it will be accepted by the majority of people alive at that time.

Sin entered our world through a lie presented by Satan, the arch liar. When speaking to religious leaders Jesus said of him,

> *"You belong to your father, the devil, and you want to carry out your father's desires. He was a murderer from the beginning, not holding to the truth, for there is no truth in him. When he lies he speaks his native language, for he is a liar and the father of lies."*
>
> John 8:44

Satan, in the guise of the snake, invaded the purity and innocence of the Garden of Eden with the first lie when he undermined what God had said, *"Did God really say. 'You must not eat from any tree in the garden'?"* (Genesis 3:1).

After sowing doubt on what God said, it was a very short step to the blatant lie presented by Satan, *"'You will not certainly die,' the snake said to the woman,"* (Genesis 3:4). Foolishly Eve (and Adam) surrendered to the word of a creature rather than obey the word of the Creator. Satan's 'take and eat' led to death and centuries later Christ's 'take and eat' were the words of salvation through Christ. Satan promised that *"their eyes would be opened and you will be like God, knowing good and evil,"* (Genesis 3:4). Almost instantly the process of death started in them, it affected their walk with God and each other and later their family. Their environment became hostile and they were ejected from their home. Acceptance of this lie affected the present and future life of Adan and Eve and has had a catastrophic effect on all of mankind.

Satan, referred to as *'that ancient snake'* in Revelation 20:2 will, through his tool, The Antichrist, present the blackest lie of all time when he will put himself forward as God, demanding to be worshipped in place of God,

> *He will oppose and will exalt himself over everything that is called God or is worshipped so that he sets himself up in God's temple, proclaiming himself to be God.*
>
> 2 Thessalonians 2:4

And so the terrible trinity of The Rebellion, The Antichrist and The Lie will be imposed on those who have the mark of the beast.

Our world is being 'softened up' in preparation for the advent of 'The Lie'. We see it in almost universal acceptance of the lie of evolution, same-sex marriage, the equality of all religions and the lie that abortion is not the greatest genocide in history. Anyone who dares to oppose total acceptance of these ideologies will be vilified, ridiculed, prosecuted and ostracised from society. It is not politically correct to question abortion, transgender rights or any other belief that the army of self-appointed censors disagree with.

The first century Thessalonian Christians faced a storm of persecution but, despite its ferocity, they were filled with an incredible joy from the Lord. They faced the wrath of unbelievers with the assurance of God's sustaining help,

> *So then, brothers and sisters, stand firm and hold fast to the teaching we passed on to you, whether by word of mouth or by letter. May our Lord Jesus Christ himself and God our Father, who loved us and by his grace gave us eternal encouragement and good hope, encourage your hearts and strengthen you in every good deed and word...the Lord is faithful, and He will strengthen you and protect you from the evil one.*
>
> 2 Thessalonians 2:15-17 and 3:3

This same 'Word-of-God' based confidence is available to all believers of all ages but will be particularly relevant for the final 'end-of-the-age' generation who will witness the appearing of Christ and the ferocious spiritual warfare that will precede it.

Part 3

Ready For His Appearing

When we come to a fresh or increased understanding of the Scriptures, it brings with it a responsibility for us to put that knowledge into practice,

> *All Scripture is God-breathed and is useful for teaching, rebuking, correcting and training in righteousness, so that the servant of God may be thoroughly equipped for every good work.*
>
> 2 Timothy 3:16

The teaching of the Thessalonian letters on the future return of Jesus must have an effect on how we live in the present. We learn so that we can be ready for His return,

> *We know that when Christ appears, we shall be like Him, for we shall see Him as He is.* ***All who have this hope in Him purify themselves, just as He is pure.***
>
> 1 John 3:2,3

The need for personal care while we wait for His coming

The stakes could not be higher, the outcome is critical; we are dealing with heaven or hell, to be with Christ or with The Antichrist, walking in the light of truth or in the darkness of Satan's deceptions, living for an eternity in the joy of the Kingdom of God or in the horror of the kingdom of darkness.

The two letters to the Thessalonians are full of teaching on the importance of being prepared for Christ's return.

In 1 Thessalonians 5:4-11, Paul warns of the danger of walking in darkness, drowsiness or drunkenness,

> *You are not in darkness (you are children of the light), let us not be like others who are asleep but let us be awake and sober. For those who sleep at night and those who get drunk get drunk at night.*

- There is no need for God's people to be in the darkness of ignorance. We have the light of God's Word which is a full and certain guide and counsel for every aspect of life.
- The followers of Christ can walk in the confidence of self-control from the Holy Ghost so they need not be inebriated or controlled by anything from the world, the flesh or the devil.
- Christ's disciples need not be surprised or terrified by any world event because they know that God is in control of this final chapter of earth's history.

Paul likens the return of Christ to the coming of a thief or the commencement of labour pains for a pregnant woman. The thief's arrival is sudden and unexpected and the woman's labour pains are not unexpected but they can start suddenly and, once started, they cannot be stopped. The return of Christ will be sudden and unexpected and once the appearing begins it will not stop until every event has happened.

So, in the closing and climactic days of these last times, we are to walk soberly, alert and self-controlled and be properly dressed for the challenge – *'let us be sober, putting on faith and love as a breastplate, and the hope of salvation as a helmet'*. All our spiritual senses must be fully alert and focussed.

Paul, Peter and Jude lay a strong emphasis on the need for personal responsibility in our readiness for Christ's return:

- *'But you, dear friends, by **building yourselves up** in your most holy faith and praying in the Holy Spirit, **keep yourselves in God's love** as you wait for the mercy of our Lord Jesus Christ to bring you to eternal life,'* (Jude v20,21).
- *'Since everything will be destroyed in this way, what kind of people ought you to be? You ought to live holy and godly lives as you look forward to the Day of God and speed its coming...**make every effort** to be found spotless, blameless and at peace with Him,'* (2 Peter 3:11,14).
- *'So then, brothers and sisters, **stand firm and hold fast** to the teachings we passed on to you,'* (2 Thessalonians 2:15).

Peter elaborates on this theme in 2 Peter 1,

> *His divine power has given us everything we need for a godly life through our knowledge of Him who called us by His own glory and goodness,* (v3).

But then he goes on to say,

> *For this very reason (the fact of what God has provided for us) **make every effort to add to your faith**...*

He then gives a list of spiritual values that we are to diligently work at developing in our lives: goodness, knowledge, self-control, perseverance etc. The basic foundation is faith, but then we are to build on what God has done in our lives, so that it's God's work complemented by our best efforts. It's not all of God or all of us, it is a partnership. Paul put it like this in 2 Timothy 1,

> *I am convinced that He is able to guard what I have entrusted to Him until that day.*

But then he added Timothy's part,

> *Guard the good deposit that was entrusted to you. Guard it with the help of the Holy Spirit who lives in us.*

It's a case of God's divine provision and power linked to our best effort in developing and strengthening our Christian walk. Peter adds the reward for those who will *"make every effort"* (he uses this phrase three times in 2 Peter),

> *If you possess these qualities in increasing measure, they will keep you from being ineffective and unproductive in your knowledge of our Lord Jesus Christ and if you do these things you will never stumble.*

Matthew 25 is a continuation of the teaching of Jesus, given in chapter 24, regarding His return at the end of the age. It contains some parables that illustrate the need for diligence while we wait for our Lord's arrival. One of the pitfalls when interpreting a parable is feeling we have to find an application for every detail in the story. Most parables have one main message with the central message in these parables being the need for watchfulness while we wait for His coming. Waiting can be a test, even dangerous, for we can become careless, lazy and lose our sense of urgency in our daily walk. Jesus made it clear that His return would be sudden and unexpected so, He warned every one of His disciples to,

Keep watch, because you do not know on what day your Lord will come.

Matthew 24:42

The parables in Matthew 24 and 25 highlight the need for watchfulness in three specific areas:

1. The parable of the servants (Matthew 24:45-51). This is a story about a wicked servant who, in the delay of his master's return, began to abuse his fellow servants only to face the wrath of his master when he returned *'on a day when he did not expect him and at an hour he was not aware of''*. His treatment of fellow workers in the waiting time was severely rebuked by his master.

2. The parable of the ten virgins (Matthew 25:1-13). This one emphasises the need for personal care. Personal neglect can result in spiritual emptiness. Five of the bridesmaids were careless and had run out of oil. Their carelessness resulted in their being excluded from the celebrations.

3. The parable of Kingdom business (Matthew 25:14-30). Some servants were entrusted with the promotion of their master's business in his absence. Most were diligent and saw the business prosper but one could not be bothered and buried his responsibility. The servants who maintained their responsibility, even while the master was absent, were rewarded and enjoyed their master's pleasure. But the one who could not be bothered and buried his responsibility had to face his master's strong displeasure.

While we are waiting for our Lord's return, we must make sure that the waiting time is not wasted time. We each have a responsibility for personal spiritual maintenance to sustain a healthy walk with the Lord. We must also exercise care in our relationships with fellow workers and not imagine that the long delay in our Lord's return gives us an excuse for abuse of other Christians. Moreover, involvement in our Master's Kingdom business is *not* an option. We each have a sphere of service which means getting down to work and not shunning it. John underlines the same message,

> *And now, dear children, continue in Him so that when He appears we may be confident and not ashamed before Him at His coming.*
>
> 1 John 2:28

Some desire to fathom out when the Day of the Lord will arrive but Jesus plainly declared,

> *It is not for you to know the times or the dates the Father has set by His own authority.*
>
> Acts 1:7

The best way is to be ready for His return at any unexpected moment, is to be living in the light of the knowledge of His return – developing a life-style of constant watchfulness in every aspect of our lives.

The reality of the Christian's warfare

When God created the heavens and the earth, He planted a garden in Eden for Adam and Eve to live in. Every possible physical need was catered for and at the close of each day they enjoyed personal fellowship with God as they walked with Him in the garden – it was co-regency,

> *God blessed* ***them*** *and said to* ***them****, 'be fruitful and increase in number; fill the earth and subdue it. Rule over the fish in the sea and the birds in the*

> *sky and over every living creature that moves on the ground'.*
>
> Genesis 1:28

Into this idyllic setting came the Tempter, in the guise of a serpent, and promised what he could not deliver,

> *"Your eyes will be opened, and you will be like God."*
>
> Genesis 3:5

By believing the serpent and yielding to his temptation, Adam and Eve surrendered their position of authority and rulership and handed it over to Satan. He is now the (temporary) ruler of this world, called *'the god of this world'* and heads up an organised opposition referred to as *'rulers of this present darkness'*. Followers of Christ live in a hostile environment, in a war zone, facing a ruthless enemy who will stoop to any depth of malice to hurt or hinder. The warfare that the Christian is involved in is primarily spiritual and the real enemies are not flesh and blood but beings from another dimension, inhabitants of the realms of darkness.

In the light of this, it is important for us to be properly dressed for this conflict – it is too early for the wedding garments (they will be needed later), but defensive armour and offensive weapons are called for; the protection of the covering that comes from truthfulness, righteousness, faith, salvation, the Word of God and prayer (see Ephesians 6). The Christians daily discipline in each of these truths is powerfully effective against all our enemies' assaults.

We have seen earlier that Peter conveyed a similar truth when he said we had to build into our lives, goodness, knowledge, self-control, perseverance, godliness, mutual affection and love, all on the foundation of our faith in Christ. Paul and Peter declared that if we will give attention and diligence to the development of these spiritual evidences in our daily lives it will stop us being ineffective, unproductive and we will be able to stand our ground against all the wiles of the devil in the evil day.

Four essential disciplines that will enable us to be ready for His return.

The early chapters of the Acts of the Apostles give us a glimpse of daily life in the first Christian Church. Peter's first sermon after Pentecost resulted in 3000 new converts joining the Church. What an amazing and exciting time it was! The daily climate of this young Church gives us a glimpse of the Kingdom of God – great grace infused everything they did, there was great power, great generosity and sharing, prayer was their daily breath, they were of one heart and one mind and everything was filled with the joy of the Lord. It would have been so easy for the young converts to just get enthralled with the daily supernatural climate but they made a determined decision to strongly commit themselves to four daily habits that would bring stability and maturity into their lives.

It is so easy to get caught up in the excitement of big meetings with powerful preachers who can capture our imaginations with wonderful stories but these four regular disciplines stand the test of time for personal benefit. These healthy habits are just as effective today and just as necessary for believers 2000 years further on. Time does not lessen their importance and the developing atmosphere of hostility to the Christian Church makes them essential habits for every Christian. The four habits are found in Acts 2:42,

> *They devoted themselves to the apostles' teaching and to fellowship, to the breaking of bread and to prayer.*

1. ***The Apostles' teaching.*** They would have access to the Old Testament books but no New Testament books had as yet been written so the apostles would re-tell the stories of Jesus – His miracles and teaching, and this would give the new converts first-hand accounts of the Lord's life and ministry. The reading and study of the whole Word of God is foundational for a life that will stand the test of opposition.

2. ***Fellowship.*** This is much more than a cup-of-tea and some chat at the end of a meeting; this is sharing life together and being willing to open up and share and receive, to give help and to receive help. This is the Body moving in harmony where every part is dependent on the other parts (see Romans 12).

3. ***The breaking of bread.*** In the context of enjoying a shared meal they would take time to lift up some broken bread to remind them of the cost of His broken body and they would partake of some wine to remind them of His shed blood. This regular habit was essential to remind believers of the cost of their salvation and to keep them walking humbly before the Lord.

4. ***Prayers.*** This was more than prayers when they had a need; this was the habit of soaking everything they did in prayer to discover God's will and ask for courage to do it. We have an example of the first century Church at prayer in Acts 4:23-31. The focus of this prayer was not for preservation or protection but power to proclaim Christ. The place shook when the Church came together to pray.

Living the Christian life is not a part-time hobby that can exist on a few spare hours per month. It has to be the full commitment of the full life devoted to the Lordship of Christ.

The Acts 2 disciples took the decision to 'devote (deliberate, focussed commitment) themselves' to four essential disciplines. The apostle could not do it for them; each one had to make their own decision to 'devote'. I cannot pay someone to do my jogging for me. If I want the benefits, I myself have to engage in the discipline.

As well as the need for personal care and attention to keep us fit for His coming, there is also a responsibility of care for our fellow believers. We are called to walk in fellowship with our Christian family and to exercise watchful care over those who may be finding the going hard.

The need for corporate care while we wait for His coming

'Am I my brother's keeper?' This was Cain's impertinent answer to God's question about his brother. The simple answer is 'yes, we are'. We do not journey to heaven in isolation, God has placed us in families, we call it Church. The Church family should care and look after all its members. In 2 Samuel 21 there is an interesting story about David who killed Goliath but later, in another war with the Philistines, he came face-to-face with another giant like Goliath and this one also had a score to settle. This time however, David was so exhausted that he faced death at the hands of this giant. Fortunately, David was not alone and one of his mighty men, Abishai, came to his rescue and killed the Philistine. We all need help from time-to-time (even the 'Davids' among us) so it is good to be in fellowship with others especially in times of danger or pressure. David's protection by Abishai underlines the truth of the verse,

> *Pity anyone who falls and has no one to help them up.*
>
> Ecclesiastes 4:10

David was safe because he was in good company.

Our care and concern for fellow believers will be expressed in different ways:

- 1 Thessalonians 5:11 – we are to encourage one another which means, endeavouring to put fresh courage into fellow believers. We are to build each other up – endeavouring to make our fellow believers bigger and stronger in their faith. The Church needs a lot more people of the Barnabas type – the apostles renamed him from Joseph to Barnabas which means, 'son of encouragement'. Hebrews 10:24,25 reminds us,

  "And let us consider how we may spur one another on towards love and good deeds, not giving up meeting together, as some are in the habit of doing, but encouraging one another – and all the more ***as you see the day approaching.***"

- In writing to the Thessalonians, Paul highlights three groups of people who needed extra help: those who are idle and disruptive – they need to be warned; those who are disheartened (timid) – they need to be given fresh heart; those who are weak – they need to be given help (1 Thessalonians 5:15).

- Care for those who are falling into sin,

  If someone is caught in a sin, you who live by the Spirit should restore that person gently. But watch yourselves, or you also may be tempted.

  Galatians 6:1

A firm response to those who deliberately walk in disobedience,

Take special note of anyone who does not obey our instructions in this letter. Do not associate with them, in order that they may feel ashamed. Yet do not regard them as an enemy, but warn them as you would a fellow believer.

2 Thessalonians 3:14,15

Closing Reflections

'Living in the light of His coming' – the challenge is to develop a life-style that is consistently ready for His appearing, remembering that it will be sudden and unexpected.

We are on the brink of unprecedented events that will take the breath away from all who will witness them. The final drama of history will be played out on the stage of the whole world and will include every living human, the entire angelic army of heaven and the demonic army of Satan. This will be Satan's last and final attempt at world domination. It will end badly for him, for along with all his fellow rebels, who carry the mark of the beast, he will be cast into the place God has prepared for his eternal incarceration (see Revelation 20).

The unbridled rage of Satan against God and His people will reach its peak as the physical appearing of Christ draws near. The three-pronged attack will be by deception, wickedness and persecution, but those who trust in God's power and are clothed by Christ's righteousness will stand firm to the end. But as well as this period of the world's history being the time of Satan's wrath, it will also be the time of God's wrath on a persistently disobedient world.

The book of Revelation records twenty-one separate judgments that will hit this world but instead of driving people to God in repentance, it will only increase their determination to defy God – very much like the response of Pharaoh and the Egyptians when God sent the plagues on

Egypt. This period of intense judgment will see plagues and events of an unprecedented magnitude – earthquakes that are off the Richter scale, hail and fire that will destroy vast areas of the earth, a third of the sea will be turned to blood, a third of the creatures in the sea will die, a third of the world's ships will be destroyed and a third of mankind will also die (Revelation 8 and 9). In these chapters you will read of hell's Abyss being opened up and releasing dreadful demonic creatures that will attack people – but only those who have the mark of the beast on them. Those who have the mark of God on their forehead will be safe from their torture. Earth will stagger from the ferocity of these judgments; people will seek death but will not be able to find it. The judgments will reach their finality when the unholy trinity of Satan, The Antichrist and the false prophet will launch their final attack on Jerusalem, amassing a coalition army that is vast, but the conflict with Satan will be a very short one. The Antichrist and the false prophet with their innumerable army will be annihilated by the fire of God.

The climate of our world towards Christians is rapidly changing. In many countries, to speak of Christ, go to Church or own a Bible carries a death penalty. Even in our own country, not to support and applaud those who have chosen a homosexual life-style, will result in persecution and sometimes prosecution. The intolerance of society for anything connected with God or His standards is rapidly increasing. The times we are entering call for a stronger expression of Church, a more confident style of leadership and members who have learned the meaning of consistent discipleship.

I once attended a seminar for leaders. The speaker was Bob Roxburgh who, at that time, was the leader of Millmead Baptist Church. He challenged us to consider three questions:

1. ***What kind of people*** are we sending out into the world? Are they discipled, trained and motivated to make a difference in their home life, work life and community life? They can appear to be great people in Church on a Sunday but it's what happens in the Monday to Saturday part that really counts.
2. ***What kind of Church*** produces people who make a difference in everyday life? Most churches have a busy weekly programme but what is all of our Church activity producing? We don't want to find that our time, energy and resources only produce wood, hay and stubble.
3. ***What kind of leadership*** produces the kind of Churches that produce the kind of people who go out into the world and make a difference?

Personal commitment

In the light of His coming and remembering the strong warning from Jesus on the effect persecution, deception and wickedness will have on many followers of Christ in the final days preceding His return, every disciple of Jesus should consider the depth of their commitment to Him. Is it settled and sure regardless of the severity of the opposition? Have you determined in your spirit that there is no point at which you could ever deny the Lord? If you are unsure, then now is the best time for you to kneel before the Lord and make that total commitment to Him.

The last words of anyone are important, so the final words from three first century leaders, speaking under the inspiration of the Holy Spirit, have something powerful to say to ***us***, the ones who may be the final generation before the coming of Jesus:

- ***Jude***

"But, dear friends, by building yourselves up in your most holy faith and praying in the Holy Spirit, keep yourselves in God's love as you wait for the mercy of our Lord Jesus Christ to bring you to eternal life."

Jude vs 20, 21

- ***Paul***

"But as for you, continue in what you have learned and have become convinced of, for you know those from whom you learned it, and how from infancy you have known the Holy Scriptures, which are able to make you wise for salvation through faith in Jesus Christ. All Scripture is God-breathed and is useful for teaching, rebuking, correcting and training in righteousness, so that the servant of God may be thoroughly equipped for every good work."

2 Timothy 3:14-17

- ***Peter***

"Therefore, dear friends, since you have been forewarned, be on your guard so that you may not be carried away by the error of the lawless and fall from your secure position. But grow in the grace and knowledge of our lord and Saviour Jesus Christ. To Him be glory both now and forever! Amen."

2 Peter 3:17,18

And Finally...

The battle is fierce and it will get fiercer but victory is assured, death will be destroyed, Satan will be eternally incarcerated and the glorious Kingdom of our Lord and Saviour will be stablished forever. The cost of involvement in this warfare is high but is nothing when compared with the glory that will follow,

> *For our light and momentary troubles are achieving or us an eternal glory that far outweighs them all. So we fix our eyes not on what is seen, but what is unseen, since what is seen is temporary but what is unseen is eternal.*
>
> 2 Corinthians 4:17,18

Stand on the truth of His Word,

To Him who is able to keep you from falling
and to present you before His glorious presence without fault and with great joy –
to the only God our Saviour be glory, majesty, power and authority, through Jesus Christ our Lord, before all ages, now and evermore!

Amen!

Other Books by Jim Dick

My Chocolate Box Journey

'Life is like a box of chocolates', so said the mother of Forrest Gump. This is the story of the light and dark flavours of life experienced in the lives of Jim and Margery Dick. This is an engaging story told with transparency and honesty. It will bring some laughter and some tears but it will inspire.

Available in hard copy (£7 plus p&p) and on Amazon Kindle.

Soul Food

A forty-day supply of refreshing insights into well-known and not-so-well known stories in the Bible – soul food for busy people.

Available in hard copy (£5 including p&p (UK)) and on Amazon Kindle.

Contact: jimdick41@gmail.com

Short Books

Available from Jim. 1-5 copies £1 each plus p&p; 6 copies or more £1 each including p&p.

Girl Power

The effective power of vision, unity and attitude. Inspiration for 21st century life from a 3000+ year-old story in the Bible.

Tell me a Story

The power of a well-told story – your story. An effective way to reach this PC generation.

Three Cheers for Leviticus

Refreshing and encouragement from the most unread book of the Bible.

Contact: jimdick41@gmail.com

On Amazon Kindle

Go to Amazon Books and type 'Jim Dick'

Heroes of Baghdad

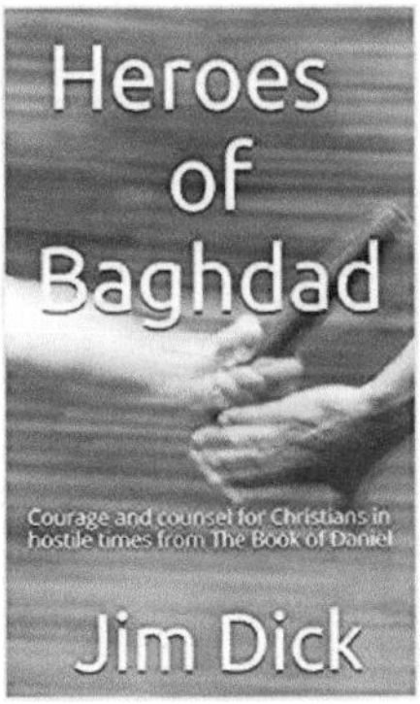

Courage and counsel for Christians living in hostile conditions from the book of Daniel – increasingly essential teaching from four young men who knew how to take a stand for God in the fires of persecution.

Success In The Secret Life

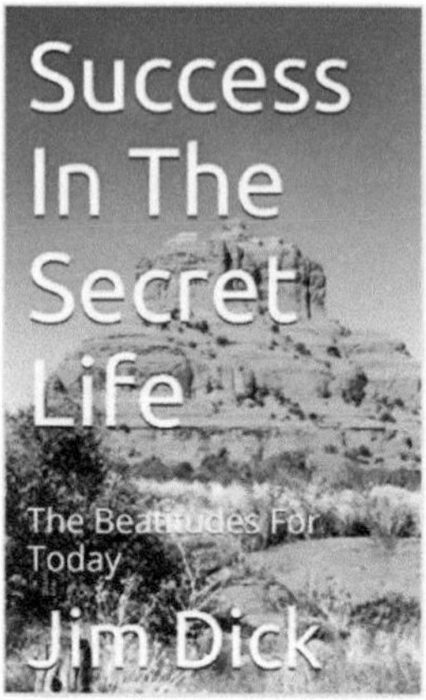

The Beatitudes for today – required reading for every believer as Jesus describes the essential attitudes and inner character of His disciples.

The Tale of Two Cities

Not London or Paris as in the Charles Dickens classic but Jerusalem and Antioch from the Acts of the Apostles. An exploration of the fatal flaw in Jerusalem that hindered it from fulfilling the Great Commission of Christ and the success factors in Antioch that made it a world-affecting Church.

9781907929892

#0040 - 120918 - C0 - 210/142/7 - PB - 9781907929892